Singing Live

The Performing Skills Guidebook for Contemporary Singers

By
Susan Anders

Published by Zanna Discs
P.O. Box 58155
Nashville, TN 37205-8155
800-787-2647
zannadiscs@bellsouth.net
www.zannadiscs.com • www.singing-live.com

Editor: Tom Manche
Cover Design: BuckinghorseDesign.com
Interior Design: Ebookgraphics.com
Photography: Trin Blakely

Table of Contents

Singing Live

Introduction

What do Elvis Presley, Eminem, Christina Aguilera, Otis Redding, John Maher, Beyoncé and Keith Urban have in common? I don't know about you, but when I see any of them perform I can't look away. Whether it's a soft intimate ballad or a high-energy screamer, they project a conviction about what they are singing that is captivating. They also make it look completely natural. What you aren't seeing are the hours of practice it took to develop that charismatic performing style.

I've coached thousands of singers: musicians and actors you've heard on the radio and seen on TV, artists and bands in development, kids, college students, heart surgeons, housewives and retirees who just loved to sing. Many of these singers would get a firm grasp on voice technique, but were either completely terrified of singing live or just didn't know how to best use their hands or the rest of their bodies when performing. From my work with them and my own work as a performer, I developed a method to guide them through the process of acquiring solid performance skills. Since I've coached singers in every contemporary style including pop, country, R&B, folk, musical theater, punk, rap, blues, jazz, and singer-songwriter, I made sure that my method was flexible enough to help these singers develop stagecraft that really worked for their particular style of music.

In the last few years we've seen the rise of many national talent search shows like *American Idol*. These shows have given singers nationwide a chance to give their singing careers a huge boost. As a result, more and more students have come to me specifically to prepare for auditions. It's one thing to win over an audience with a forty-minute set, and a whole other skill to win over a judge in sixty seconds. Even if you aren't aiming to be the next *American Idol, a*uditioning is a part of life for most singers. Because of this, I've included a great deal of information on how to prepare and deliver a standout audition.

Good performing isn't just how well you do when the curtain rises or when your name is called at the audition. It's knowing yourself inside out as an artist so that everything you do on stage is powerful *and* authentic. It's knowing how to dissect and dive into a lyric to make the song completely your own. It's knowing how to handle stage fright and how to stay focused and positive. It's having practical knowledge like good mic technique, how to talk to a sound person, how to find songs that really complement you as an artist, what to say in-between songs, and how to pace a set. You'll learn all of these skills in this book.

I've lived in music industry towns for the last eighteen years, first in Los Angeles and now in Nashville. As a result, I've worked with many extremely talented singers who came to these cities to make their mark. They need to not just be great singers, but to really stand out among the crowd of other hopefuls. For them, for my other students, and for myself I've studied everything that can make a performer really shine. In this book I pass that information on to you.

How To Use This Book

There are two good ways to use this book. The first way is to simply read through the book and do all of the exercises in order. You'll start with some preparatory goal and stage persona defining work, move on to song preparation and performance rehearsals, and end with actual performances.

The second way to work is to do your preparatory goal and stage persona defining work at the same time as you practice your songs. You can clean up any technical issues the song may have and refine your vocal delivery and interpretation while you are doing the earlier exercises.

Either one of these approaches is fine. Just remember to complete all of the preparatory work before you start the actual performance exercises.

If you are extremely nervous about performing for other people, work through the book as slowly as you need to. The preparatory work you do will give you a much better understanding of yourself as a performer, which will help to ground you. The progression of the exercises allows you to gradually refine and develop your confidence as a performer without an audience. That confidence will help carry you along as you venture into actual performances. The chapters on handling nerves and preparing yourself mentally will also ease the way.

I recommend that you copy the pages with exercises so you can write on them and keep notes. Writing everything down will keep you focused. I also recommend that you commit to a regular practice schedule and mark it in your calendar. There's more on that in the *Performance Goals* chapter.

If you have an upcoming performance you should rehearse daily if at all possible. Daily practice, even for short periods of time, can instill habits that will stay with you. If daily practice is impossible, try to do some performance work two to four times a week, and sing daily.

If you have an audition happening very soon, go directly to the *Song Selection* chapter and start there. Also read Chapter 6, *Vocal Technique & Delivery*, Chapter 8, *Focus*, and especially Chapter 17, *Audition Preparation*. When you have time later on, go back to the beginning and do all the exercises from the earlier chapters. This will give you a better foundation for future auditions and other performances.

Tools you'll need

- A calendar or datebook for scheduling rehearsals.

- A large mirror, preferably full-length, in your bedroom/rehearsal space.

- A camcorder, DVD camera, or other way to film yourself. Though not absolutely essential, this is an invaluable tool. If you can't afford one, ask friends if they have one you can borrow. Also see if a local school or church might have one you can use. Throughout this book I'll use the term videotape to mean any of the various ways you can film yourself.

- Backing tracks if you don't play an instrument. These can be karaoke CDs or piano/guitar tracks. If you are in a band, try to get a recording of some of your songs minus your vocal. You'll also need something to play the tracks on: boombox, stereo, etc. Do not use CDs with someone else singing! You can find lots of karaoke versions of songs on Itunes for 99 cents each. Even if you are preparing for an a cappella audition it's smart to start with a backing track to solidify your pitch and rhythm.

- Some way to record yourself and your backing tracks as you prepare your song for the performance exercises. This doesn't have to be elaborate or expensive. At one point in my studies I played my backing tracks on a boombox and recorded myself singing with the tracks onto a cheap cassette recorder. It wasn't high fidelity but it got the job done.

Optional tools

- A notebook for writing additional answers to any of the exercises and for taking notes about your rehearsals and performances.

- A mic, mic stand and a way to amplify yourself. Some options include:

- Home karaoke machines with mics (get a stand, too)— these are good because you can play your backing track on them as well.

- Home stereo systems: some older receivers have a mic input— you can plug a mic into it and sing through your stereo speakers. If your receiver doesn't have a mic input you can get a small 4-channel mixer— connect your mic to it, then connect the mixer to your stereo receiver and sing through your speakers. You will also need to connect your backing track through the mixer. That could be your instrument or a tape or CD player. www.sweetwater.com and www.musiciansfriend.com are both good sites for doing research on this, plus they have a support staff who can advise you via phone or email.

- PA systems: If you're in a band and have a set rehearsal space, or if you're a performer who plays lots of venues that don't have sound systems, a PA can be worth owning. But don't run out and buy one yet, it may not be right for your goals as a performer. Many pro performers worked on their performance chops at home, practiced their mic technique with a hairbrush, then got comfortable with sound systems when they started doing open mic nights or casual gigs.

What you won't find in this book

Though I'll be writing about evaluating and polishing your vocal performances, information on how to improve your voice technique isn't covered here. If you need more work on singing technique before focusing on your performance chops, please check out one of my vocal warm up and technique methods, either Volumes One or Two of the No Scales Just Songs Vocal Workout http://www.singersworkout.com or Singing with Style http://www.singingwithstyle.com.

Chapter 1:
Components of a Great Performance

Your performance is the combination of everything that happens when you are on stage:

- The songs you sing
- The musical arrangement of the songs
- Your execution of those songs
- How you move your body
- Everything you say in-between songs
- Your demeanor

All of these factors, which are within your control, influence an element of a performance that you *can't* completely control: the energy. That's the atmosphere in the room created by the synergy between the audience and the performer. When an artist performs well and the audience responds to them, a potent energy is created that is wonderful to experience. That's the "performance high": experiencing great performance energy that you know you helped to create.

But you can't control that energy any more than you can force Johnny Depp or Beyoncé to fall in love with you. Think of all the talented artists who have opened for big acts. They could fly across the stage and still not impress an impatient audience waiting to see the headliner. The audience response is the chaos factor that's part of every performance an artist gives.

When all the elements go well, the performance is magic. We performers eat that up like candy, and it's why we spend so much time rehearsing, analyzing and polishing our craft.

As you work your way through this book you will be thinking a lot about great performances: ones you've seen, ones you hope to give, and perhaps ones you've already given. There are many components to delivering a fantastic performance, including:

- **Craft, both vocal and stagecraft**. Singers practice, and then practice some more to develop vocal power, control and finesse. Performing singers also learn the elements of stagecraft, including focus, how their body movements can best convey a song, and stage patter. When a performer masters both music and stagecraft they experience a boost in...

- **Confidence**. We've all seen performers who owned the stage and seemed to hold the audience in the palm of their hand. That ability comes from performers with a high level of vocal and stagecraft mastery and subsequent confidence in themselves. Another component of confidence is...

- **Mental attitude**. Learning to maintain a positive mental attitude helps a performer focus and transcend mental and external distractions that can disrupt a performance. When a performer has a positive mental attitude, a high level of vocal and stagecraft mastery, and his confidence is high, he may experience...

- **Flow**. Some performers experience this as a feeling of great control, as if they are juggling ten balls with complete confidence. Some feel it almost as an out-of-body experience, some feel that time slows down. Flow is the ultimate performance high. It can be a rare occurrence for some performers but is something for which we all strive.

Chapter 2:
Performance Goals

You need to know what your goals are as a singer before you can develop an authentic performing style. A singer whose goal is to front a heavy metal band will need a very different style than someone who wants to sing Beatles songs with an acoustic guitar at coffeehouses. So the first thing to do is get clear on your dreams and goals as a singer.

Haven't we all daydreamed about performing, perhaps while standing in line at the bank or walking the dog? Now I want you to daydream in a more focused way. Make sure you won't be disturbed for a few minutes. Get comfortable, sitting or lying down. Take a few deep breaths, then imagine yourself singing for an audience somewhere. It can be in a tiny coffeehouse or an arena. You can be on TV or live. You can have one pianist, the Boston Pops Orchestra or Led Zeppelin backing you up. Imagine the most fun and satisfying situation you can.

If you're having trouble thinking of something, then try out some different scenarios by imagining yourself singing in the following situations:

- Dressed in faded jeans, wailing with a loud rock band to an audience of 5,000 screaming fans.
- Dressed in an evening gown or tuxedo, singing jazz standards with a piano-bass-drums trio in a downtown club to an audience of appreciative upscale music lovers.
- Just you and your guitar, playing your original songs at a small concert hall to an audience who hang on your every word.
- Belting out your number one R&B song, singing and dancing across the stage at the Grammies.

Feel free to change these scenarios as much as you like, it's your daydream!

Daydreaming to Define Your Goals

After you've imagined a performance scenario that feels right, answer these questions:

1. What style of music are you singing?

2. What are you wearing?

3. Where are you— arena, coffeehouse, on Conan O'Brien?

4. What kind of accompaniment do you have? Full orchestra, power trio, beatbox, acoustic guitar?

You began to clarify your style as a performer with this last exercise. Now I want you to find some role models with a similar style. Here are some examples. Let's say your answers in Exercise #1 were this:

Style: country
Clothes: jeans and t-shirt
Location: arena
Accompaniment: rocking band

Some artists that fit this are:
Garth Brooks, Tim Mcgraw, and Dixie Chicks

Here's another set of answers:
Style: soulful singer-songwriter
Clothes: casual chic
Location: large theater
Accompaniment: acoustic guitar
Artists that fit:
Corinne Bailey Rae, Shawn Colvin, Ben Harper, and John Maher

What if your answers don't really fit a style you've seen before? Here's an example:

Style: punk
Clothes: tuxedo
Location: Saturday Night Live
Accompaniment: bongos

This artist is pretty original and will definitely stand out! When looking for artist role models, look at eclectic artists, punk rockers AND performers who wear tuxedos. Therefore:

Artists: Sex Pistols (punk), k.d. lang (tuxedo), and Beck (eclectic)

Performer Role Models

List four artists that somewhat fit the description you created in the previous exercise.

1.
2.
3.
4.

These questions are to help you define your goals as a performer and also to help you find some role models to use as you evaluate your own performing style. Remember, Prince and Norah Jones are both great performers, but they have very different performing styles. No one is going to judge Norah's dance moves, and Prince would probably get depressed if his audience sat as quietly rapt as the audience at a Norah Jones concert. There's nothing wrong with studying artists whom you don't see as role models. I think you can learn from every good performer out there regardless of musical style. But I want you to have some artists who are in the ballpark of what you want to do as a performer. Years ago my rock band broke up and I began performing solo with just as acoustic guitar. The bigger, more dramatic moves that had worked with my band were way too theatrical for my new persona. So I studied a slew of acoustic singer-songwriters and stole everything I could from the best of them.

Keep adding to your list of performer role models whenever you see one that inspires you. You'll be using this list later.

Goal setting

Now let's look at some specific performance goals. You may see yourself playing Carnegie Hall in three years, but you'll get more motivated if you pick some short-term goals. You can break down your performance goals into two sets. The first set includes your goals that fit a time frame. Make these goals specific. "Improve my vocal range in three months" is too general, while "Able to sing high C in three months" *is* specific. Suppose you are a singer who has never been in a band, has very little performance experience and is pretty nervous about that. You may set yourself the goal of joining a band in one year. Work backwards from that point and make a list of goals that will prepare you for that. A list of short-term goals might look like this:

- Month #1: Read the first four chapters in this book. Do all the exercises. Get clear on my goals, intention, role models, and persona.
- Month #2: Pick three songs to rehearse and get backing tracks for them. Learn them.
- Month #3: Iron out any technical problems with the songs.
- Month #4: Work focus and body movements in mirror and on video. Polish my performance of the three songs. Create list of people I can use as my 'safe' audience OR form or join a performance group or class.
- Month #5: Sing 1-3 of the songs for a trusted friend.
- Month #6: Sing at a karaoke club.
- Month #7: Continue karaoke singing and home rehearsal, analyzing and improving my performances.
- Month #8: Continue karaoke practice and look for bands that need singers on Craigslist, Myspace, etc. (For help with this, see my article called "How To Find Musicians" here: http://www.zannadiscs.com/srarticle_6.html)

- Month #10: Continue karaoke practice, contact and audition for bands.
- Month #11: Join a band

This could all change, of course. Along the way you may decide to form your own band, you may get the flu and stop singing for a month, or you may fall in love and move to Paris. You can always make adjustments to roll with the changes life brings. But the act of writing down your goals keeps you focused and on track. Studies have shown that the most successful people have specific goals and write them down.

Let's say your goal is to audition for *American Idol* or a similar talent search show in early August and it's now April. Your short-term goals might look like this:

- By April 15th: Find a great audition song and at least one back-up song. Research and read all of the *American Idol* audition advice on the internet.
- By May 1st: Memorize the song(s) and practice them with and without a backing track. (If possible learn the whole song, though you'll probably just do a portion of it at the audition. This way you can also practice it at karaoke clubs.)
- By May 15th: Handle all vocal technique issues. Analyze intention, lyric analysis, and back-story. (These topics will all be discussed later in the book.)
- By June 1st: Solidify focus, all gestures and body moves with mirror work.
- By June 15th: Start videotaping. Perfect performance. Practice mental preparation.
- By July 1st: A cappella performance for a 'safe' friend.
- By July 15th: A cappella performances for anyone who will 1) sit still for a minute, and 2) not give negative feedback unless asked for it.
- Early August: Hit the audition.

Specific Goal Setting

Now it's your turn:

Name the primary goal you have as a singer and put the date you could see it happening:

Now break your goals down into 8-12 smaller goals. If your goal is a year from now break your smaller goals into months, If it's two months from now break it down into weeks, etc.

1.	
2.	
3.	
4.	
5.	
6.	
7.	
8.	
9.	
10.	
11.	
12.	

If you like, you can break these short-term goals into smaller, more doable tasks. Be precise. It's much easier to do something specific like "Look on Craigslist for bands seeking singers" than the vaguer "Find a band to join."

Ongoing goals

Besides progressing towards one's ultimate goal, singers must also carve out some time for daily practice. This includes a vocal warm up and then practicing your songs as much as possible. I call these "ongoing goals." Some singers will warm up on their way to work or as they do the dishes in the morning, then practice songs later in the day. Warming up while doing something else isn't ideal, but it's better than not warming up at all. If you can get into a ritual of warming up at the same time every day you are more apt to do it regularly.

You'll want to sing songs as well as exercises to maintain your voice technique, so set aside some time for that. Ideally your technique should be so solid that you don't have to think much about it during rehearsals, freeing you to focus on the many other aspects of performing.

Pull out your calendar and take a minute to look at your week ahead. Is there time to warm up for 10-20 minutes almost every day? If you have a regular work or school schedule, see how your vocal practice can fit into it. If you have trouble remembering to practice, mark some times in your calendar when you can do this. If you have broken your long-term goals into smaller tasks you can jot those down too.

While you're at it, write 'goals' on every Sunday or Monday in your calendar. That will remind you to evaluate how well you've kept to your schedule the previous week, and to schedule the following week's rehearsals. You can also look at the short and long-term goals you wrote down in the previous exercise to see if you are on track.

Try to be reasonable as you schedule your ongoing goals. If you schedule every spare minute for rehearsal and nothing else you risk burning out. Leave time for family, friends, ample sleep and even some time to space out a bit.

Ongoing Goal Setting

List your ongoing musical goals. Examples: 15 minutes of vocal warm-up daily, 3 one-hour performance rehearsals weekly.

1.
2.
3.
4.

Maybe you are a disciplined person who practices regularly and doesn't need reminders, but most of us need a little help. I have been in several 'goals groups' of two to four people who met regularly to keep each other on track and brainstorm when one of us hit a real or emotional block. These get-togethers can be as simple as a ten-minute check-in during your coffee break at work, or as comprehensive as a three-hour meeting. The point is to meet regularly and keep each other accountable.

Chapter 3:
Intention

Powerful performers have very clear intentions about how they want their audience to feel. I'm guessing that Usher wants his audience to be aroused (among other things), Trisha Yearwood wants her audience to be moved, Enya wants her audience to be soothed, Bob Dylan wants you to think, and Weird Al Yankovic wants you to laugh. Your intentions as a performer will influence your choice of material, how you dress, how you move, how you connect with the audience— every aspect of your performance.

Now that you've solidified some of your short and long-term goals as a performer, let's go back to the focused daydreaming you did for this next exercise.

Clarifying Your Intentions

Think about the audience you were singing to as you daydreamed about your ideal performance situation and answer these questions:

1. How does your audience feel as they hear you? Check any of these that apply:

Inspired _____
Revved up _____
Moved _____
Amused _____
Angry _____
Impressed and awed _____
Like they are with their best friend _____
Jarred or disturbed _____
Turned on _____

Entertained _____
Connected to God _____

List any other emotions you would like your audience to feel when they hear and see you perform:

2. What is your audience *doing*: screaming, listening intently, dancing, crying, clapping along, or singing along?

Your answers here will help you clarify your intentions as a performer. Once your intention is clear to you, everything about your performance will be easier to practice and evaluate. Performers who are unclear on their underlying intention can be unfocused, nervous, and scattered. Of course, within a set or even within one song you may have several intentions. Green Day would probably like their audience to be inspired, revved up, moved, amused, angry *and* entertained at some point during their shows. It's fine and probably good to want your audience to feel a multitude of feelings, but try to get specific on what those different feelings are.

Spend some more time thinking about what you want your audience to think, feel and do during your performance. When you are clear on your intentions, look at your list of role models from the previous chapter and see if you think they have similar intentions. Revise or add to your list of role models so that you include artists who have similar intentions to yours.

Chapter 4:
Stage Persona

The importance of knowing your stage persona

Your stage persona is the character you become when you are on stage. André 3000 of OutKast's stage persona is a flamboyant, wild, fun-loving guy. Many people don't realize that in real life he is a soft-spoken, thoughtful vegetarian.

Your stage persona can be very close to who you are in real life or someone completely different. There's no right or wrong here. What's important is to have a clear vision of what your persona is. When I was first performing I struggled with how I wanted to act on stage. Finally I realized that I wanted to be a slightly larger-than-life version of how I am (or at least hope I am) in real life: down-to-earth, funny and smart. Before that, I was trying much too hard to be sexy and distant. Once I determined the stage persona that worked for me, performing became a whole lot easier.

If you think of just about any powerful performer you'll notice that each one has a strong, definable persona. For example, Josh Turner is a down-to-earth boy next door. Marilyn Monroe was a sexy seductress. Rocker Henry Rollins is a smart, angry, primal guy. Queen Latifah is like your cool big sister who is relaxed and confident.

Coming up is the first of several research exercises, where you'll be studying different performers to analyze different aspects of his or her performing style. For all of the research exercises you can watch performances live, on TV, on DVD, or on Youtube or similar sites. Highly edited music videos with lots of special effects may not be the best ones for study purposes. Remember that you can learn a lot from bad performances, too. As you work through the exercises you'll find that you are analyzing other performances in more depth. This will help you immensely as you polish your own performance skills.

Stage Persona Research

Spend an hour watching different performances on Youtube, or go see four local performers, either bands or soloists. Notice which performers are compelling, and which ones have strong personas. Are the most interesting performers the best singers, or is there something else about them that you like? If you see a bad performance, notice whether the performer has a definable persona.

For this next exercise, you can think about any of the performances you viewed during your research, or just think about some other powerful performers.

Stage Persona Defining

List five compelling performers and their personas, for example:

Performer: Josh Turner   Persona: Down-to-earth boy-next-door

Performer	Persona
1.	
2.	
3.	
4.	
5.	

By now you've given some thought to what a stage persona is, you've seen some in action, and you've identified some effective ones. Now it's time to define your own persona.

Think again about how you saw yourself performing during your focused daydreaming. What kind of person were you watching? Slick or grungy? Theatrical or unaffected? Friendly or abrasive?

Your intention should offer a big clue. If you want your audience to be in awe of you, then you want to be a larger-than-life character. If you want them to want to see you as a drinking buddy, then your persona is more down-to-earth. If you want them to lust after you, then being seductive is part of your persona. Remember that your persona can have many different elements: Prince is sexy, mysterious, flirtatious, charismatic *and* insightful.

If you still draw a blank, think about one of your performing role models and try to describe his or her persona. Does this sound like what you want to be? Another thing you can do if you're stuck is to figure out what you *don't* want to be and work from there. Write down some aspects of performers you hate ("too theatrical, too introverted, too giggly") and use those to help define what you want your performance persona to be.

Defining Your Stage Persona

Describe your stage persona in ten words or less:

It's very important to get a clear idea of your stage persona, but if you really get stuck on this exercise you can read on and come back to it later. You may find that it begins to gel as you do more of the exercises in this book. Also keep in mind that your persona may change over time. Madonna has moved through many personas during her long career, including wild bohemian, glamour girl, and sex queen.

Chapter 5:
Song Selection

By now you should have a good idea of your goals and intentions as a performer as well as your stage persona. The next step is to make sure that your songs are ready. What do I mean by ready? Three things: first, you need to examine the songs you're singing to ensure they are right for you. Secondly, your voice technique needs to be solid on each song so that you are free to focus all of your attention on your performance. And finally, you'll need to have a thorough understanding of the song lyrics so you can deliver them with authenticity. Let's look at song selection first.

If you haven't yet picked songs you want to perform, now's the time to start looking. Stay in the style you want to sing. If you want to be a country singer, use country songs, etc. Though it's valuable sometimes to step outside the style where you see yourself, it'll be easier to feel authentic in your preferred style.

How many songs to pick for the exercises

Most singers should pick two or three songs to use for performance exercises. If you're prepping for a big audition where only one is required it's fine to focus on one, but keep in mind that it's always good to have a second song prepared for auditions, just in case. A student of mine was asked to sing three different songs during the first round of the *American Idol* auditions even though 99% of the contestants only sing one song.

Even if you're in a band that does a set of a dozen songs, it will be easier to start with just two or three. You can apply what you've learned to other songs later on. From here on out I'll refer to "your song" with the assumption that you are actually preparing two or three.

Matching your song to your performing goals, intention and persona

Once you've picked two or three songs, examine them to see if they fit your performing goals, intention and persona. You probably shouldn't sing "Hit Me With Your Best Shot" if you are an intellectual folk singer. You probably shouldn't sing "Why Don't We Do It In The Road?" if you are an inspirational gospel singer. Do a quick analysis of each song to make sure it fits your vision. You'll be doing a more detailed analysis later.

Think about your intention. If you want your audience to be moved pick a moving song. If you want them to stand up and dance pick a song with a serious groove. If you want them to laugh pick a funny song. Don't pick a song just because you like it, make sure that it will serve your intentions as a performer.

Now think about your stage persona. Does your song complement it or conflict with it?

It's fine and perhaps beneficial to work with two very different songs in order to show different parts of your persona. After her single "Don't Forget to Remember Me" came out, Carrie Underwood's audience thought of her as a sweet young thing. She followed that with the gutsy, fiery "Before He Cheats," which showed a whole other side to her persona and established her as a star. Clearly her persona could encompass two very different sides.

Other song selection considerations

If you are preparing for performances where you can only sing one or two songs, like auditions, open mic nights and karaoke nights, make sure to pick a song that shows you off. You want to stand out and be noticed amidst other singers. Avoid overdone songs that everyone has heard way too many times before, and avoid the latest hits since they will be too familiar and closely identified with the artist who sings them.

Find a song that is easy enough to sing that you sound good, but is challenging enough that it shows what you can do.

Find a song that works with the tone (also called timbre) of your voice. Singers with sweet, airy voices will sound weird singing heavy metal screamer songs. Compare the tone of your voice to those of your role models and make sure that it's in the ballpark.

Technical considerations

What is the song's range?

Make sure you can reach all of the highest and lowest notes without straining. Some songs may be too rangy for you in any key, but if just the low *or* high notes are a problem you can sing it in a different key than the original. If you're working with a prerecorded track you're stuck in that one key. If you're singing a cappella, or are accompanying yourself, experiment until you find a key that works for you. Some karaoke machines and other devices can change the key.

If you can't sing all of the highest and lowest notes without straining, consider another song. Keep in mind that when the adrenaline of performing hits, a singer's range can shift higher. Many singers find in performance that they can sing a whole step or more higher than when singing at home. However, usually in this case the lowest notes in a singer's range become very difficult to sing. You may find when you start rehearsing in front of real people that you'll need to adjust the key of your song higher to account for this phenomenon.

How physically demanding is the song?

Can you sing the entire song without experiencing vocal fatigue? Fatigue shows up as discomfort in your throat or hoarseness. You're going to be singing this song over and over, so make sure it won't wear you out.

Also, you should love the song you've picked. There are songs that really hold up to repeated performances and ones that get old. As you look at your song more deeply during the next few exercises you may realize that it doesn't hold up. Be willing to toss it and find another one.

Song Selection

List your 2-3 songs here:

1.
2.
3.

Chapter 6:
Vocal Technique & Delivery

After you've selected, learned and memorized a song, the easiest way to tell if it is performance-ready is to record yourself singing it and then listen back. A cheap cassette deck is fine if you don't have a fancy recording set-up or an application like Garageband on your computer.

Vocal technique issues to evaluate

1. **Notes:** Are they all there? I know that sounds funny, but some singers will skip the highest notes or slide over the fast notes.

2. **Rhythm & Tempo:** Are you consistently singing with the beat or are you occasionally ahead or behind it?

3. **Breathing:** If you aren't pacing yourself with regular and deep singer breaths, your tone could deteriorate as the song progresses. You may go off-key, and numerous other problems may arise. Though ideally you'll be so well-rehearsed that you won't need to think about technique when performing, the one thing you may need to monitor when you're on stage is your breathing.

4. **Tone:** Is your tone pleasing? Throat tension and other voice problems will show up as an edgy, strained, or overly breathy tone. Good voice technique improves your tone quality.

5. **Intonation:** Are you in tune or do you sound like you are singing some of the notes flat or sharp (under or above the correct pitch)? Poor intonation, or being "pitchy," is one of the biggest problems singers have, especially with the pressures of singing live. It's worth the time to make sure you sing in tune before moving forward. Good intonation goes hand-in-hand with the following:

6. **Accuracy:** Are you scooping up to notes instead of hitting them dead-on? Are you falling off the last note or slurring over the last few notes at the ends of phrases? Good singers strive to maintain a balance of accurate notes and flowing phrases. Too much accuracy and you'll sound mechanical; too much sliding and the notes will be indistinct. How much accuracy versus how much flow varies from style to style. If you aren't sure, listen to some other singers in your style of music and compare their delivery to yours.

7. **Vowels:** Your voice projects and sustains on vowel sounds, not consonants. Do your vowels sound natural for your style of music? It's fine to have a twang if you're singing country, and it's fine to sound southern if you're singing the blues. Listen to other singers in your musical style and notice how they pronounce words, particularly on sustained notes. Compare their vowel pronunciation to yours.

8. **Articulation:** Vowels project the sound but consonants are important too. Can you understand each word? How much to articulate varies from style to style. Some blues and rock singers are pretty relaxed with their articulation, but these days I hear fairly crisp articulation in most R&B, folk, country, pop, rap and acoustic music singers. If you choose to sing with relaxed articulation make it a conscious choice, not a sloppy accident. It's much easier to hear dropped consonants when you aren't singing, so listen to your recorded vocal and circle any problem consonants on your lyric sheet for later rehearsal. Listen especially to how well you articulate Ns, Ds, NDs, and NGs, and listen for the last consonant of each phrase. It's also possible to over-articulate your consonants, which can cause you to sound robotic and over-trained. Good diction should sound natural.

9. **Delivery:** Are you singing note-by-note or phrase-by-phrase? The latter usually sounds better. What happens at the ends of your phrases? Do you let your vibrato come in as you hold and fade on the last note or do you hold the note strong and loud and then cut it off? Either one is a legitimate delivery choice, just make sure that they are what you choose to sing. The more

awareness you have of your delivery choices, the more vocal control you'll have during a performance.

10. **Dynamics:** Is the song all at the same volume or does it have dynamics? A common use of dynamics is to have softer verses that build into louder choruses. How about dynamics within a phrase; is every word at the exact same volume level? That might sound unnatural. Do you swell or fade on sustained notes? Dynamics are a powerful tool that every singer should be aware of and use.

11. **Stylizing:** Do you need to experiment with phrasing, runs, ornaments and dynamics to make the song more your own? Whether you stylize a lot, a little bit, or not at all is your personal artistic choice, but it's worth looking at as you evaluate your vocals.

As I mentioned earlier, this book doesn't go into vocal stylizing or vocal technique in depth. If you feel that any of these areas may be the missing link to your giving a good performance, by all means look into my or someone else's instructional materials. I've often had students study vocal technique with me for months before we started preparing for performances.

Evaluating Your Vocal Technique

Record yourself singing your song until you have a version you like. Then evaluate it with this checklist.

Song Title: _____

Grade these elements of your vocal performance on a scale of 1 to 10, 10 being excellent.

1. Notes _____
2. Rhythm & tempo _____
3. Breathing _____
4. Tone quality _____
5. Intonation _____
6. Accuracy _____
7. Vowels _____
8. Articulation _____
9. Delivery _____
10. Dynamics _____
11. Stylizing _____

Some additional tips for polishing your vocals

1. **Break bad habits:** If you repeat the same mistake over and over you have probably 'learned the mistake.' That means your body has memorized how the mistake feels and just does it automatically. One way to disrupt this cycle is to practice slowly so that you can anticipate and interrupt the automatic error.

2. **Isolate problems:** Don't sing an entire song over and over if just one or two phrases are where you have problems. Work just one phrase until it's right, then sing the section that includes the

phrase. Then try adding the section before it and so on until you can do the entire song correctly.

3. **Take notes:** Once you've isolated any problems, jot the solutions down on your lyric sheet. These might be something like: "Breathe before the final high note," "Go softer on the bridge," or "Articulate the last 'D' of the final phrase." Before you rehearse your song the next day check your notes. Too often singers forget what they've rehearsed the day before and repeat the same mistake when they return to the trouble spot.

4. **Scan ahead:** During long pauses or instrumental breaks mentally prepare for what's up ahead. Many songs have easier verses followed by killer choruses— enjoy those easy verses, but don't get lulled into a state of false confidence. Anticipate the more difficult passages so they don't take you by surprise.

If you really hate what you're hearing, don't be discouraged. You may need to work with a voice coach to improve your voice before worrying about performances, but you may just need to spend more time singing on your own, focusing on various items on the checklist. Work on one area at a time so you don't get overwhelmed— you may spend a great deal of time working through this checklist. If you want to work on your performance and vocal technique at the same time you can combine this vocal work with any research exercises that come after this chapter. If you do read ahead while polishing your vocal, just do the research exercises and leave the actual performance rehearsals for later.

Recording one's voice is necessary for the evaluation process, but during my own practice sessions I've discovered an additional benefit. I find that just hitting the red button and knowing that I'm being recorded gets my adrenaline flowing and makes me a bit nervous, just like when I'm performing. Perfecting my vocals in that state of heightened awareness prepares me for the adrenaline rush of an actual performance.

Chapter 7:
Lyric Study

Why lyric study is important

We've all heard singers "phone in" a song, where they sound fine but something seems to be missing. That something is usually the singer's connection with the song. You can't be connected if you don't know what the song is about!

I once studied with the late great voice teacher Judy Davis, who taught Barbra Streisand. She said, "When you're performing, about 5% of your attention should be on your accompaniment so you stay in tune. The other 95% of your attention should be on what you are saying at that moment." That means there's one more area of preparation to work on before you begin your performance exercises: lyric study. This one element can make the difference between a good and a great performance.

Lyric Analysis

Pick one of your songs, read through the lyrics and ask yourself the following questions. Do this even if you wrote the song and think you know the answers. Notice that these are the classic "who, what, when, where, and why" questions that writers ask themselves as they flesh out a story.

Song Title: _____

1. Who is singing this song? Are they male or female, young or old, rich or poor, trucker or physicist?

2. <u>What</u> is the context? Did someone break their heart, did they just travel the world, did they just get home from work?

3. <u>When</u> is the song being sung? morning, 5 PM, 4 AM? During a hectic workday or on a relaxed Sunday afternoon?

4. <u>Where</u> is the singer? In a car, in bed, at work, on a beach, on a stage talking to an audience?

5. <u>Why</u> is the singer singing this song? To tell a story, to celebrate joy, to express despair?

6. <u>How</u> does the singer feel? Is he or she ecstatic, angry, yearning? Does that mood evolve as the song progresses?

I want you to analyze the lyric until you have a crystal clear idea of the character and his point of view, as well as the setting and context for the song. This will make your performance more believable. You're studying the lyric the way an actor studies her lines, looking for her character's motivation.

What if your song is a light "Hey, let's get up and dance" kind of song, do you still need to do a lyric analysis? Yes, and here's why: you don't know what your emotional state will be when you perform a song. You may have had a lousy sound check, you may be worrying about money, or your boyfriend may have just dumped you right before the show (this happened to me years ago!) You'll need every trick in the book to authentically sing a happy "Let's dance!" song if you've had an awful day. Knowing the who-what-when-where-why of every song you perform will help you get to the essence of each song quickly. This is also helpful if you're performing a set of songs that vary in mood.

Finding visual and sensory cues for your song

Some singers like to visualize their own little movie of what's happening as they sing. Other singers rely on sensory cues to get into the right frame of mind. Here are some examples: imagining the coffee smell for a song that happens in a coffee shop, imagining the splash of raindrops if it's a rainy day song, or imagining a lover's touch for a bedroom song.

Some people are more visual, some are more aural (what you hear), and some are more kinesthetic (what you feel). It's useful to figure out which way you lean since that can help you pick more effective cues. Think about the last party you went to and how you would describe it to a friend. If you'd say something like "The room was gold and everyone was wearing shiny clothes" then you may be more visual. If you'd say something like "I was feeling very amped up and excited as I walked into the room," that's a "feeling" statement and you may be more kinesthetic. If you say "the first thing I noticed was the jazz music playing and all the chattering voices" then you may be more aural. Use that knowledge to pick cues that are easy for you to remember and hook into.

If you are rehearsing several songs it can be helpful to jot down a few cue phrases to help you dive into the meaning and mood of the song each time you come back to it. These can be words that evoke the scene, like "2 a.m. Monday" or "Right after the first date," emotional cues like "bittersweet" or "desperate," sensory cues like "hot and sweaty," or less obvious cues that pull you into the song like "bright yellow," "grainy," or "like a back alley in the rain." The point is to have a few words that swiftly bring back to you all of the homework you did on the lyric. If a drunk woman keels over right in front of you during a performance (this has happened to me) you'll need to refocus on what you're singing about, and you won't have time to review your entire back-story, imagery, etc. A few easy triggers can help you do that.

Some singers skip the cues and just focus on the lyrics and the emotions they evoke. The important thing is to know what's going on in the song so you aren't just repeating some lines someone wrote.

When lyrics are vague

Many song lyrics are vague about what is going on, or are very open to interpretation. If that's the case with your song, make up a set of who-what-when-where-whys and sensory cues that work for you. It doesn't matter if you know that the song was written about a cat that ran away and your back-story is about a bad breakup. If your back-story hooks you into the song, use it. If the song is so vague or poetic that there is no clear meaning to the words, get a feel for the mood of the song and simply make up a back-story that works with that mood.

Sometimes analyzing a song reveals just a couple of lines that don't make sense. Your choice then is to ignore the bad logic and focus on the story as a whole as you sing those lines, or rewrite the offending line. The latter won't please the songwriter, but it happens.

The emotional feel of a song is open to interpretation: You get to decide. You can try on different emotions, sensory cues and back-stories as you practice until you find one that feels right. For example, I've heard the old standard "Happy Days Are Here Again" sung with complete joy and also as a tentative, hopeful ballad.

If you aren't convinced that creating a back-story and finding sensory cues for every song you perform is important, here's one more reason: fighting nerves. Nervous singers become very self-conscious as the panic sets in. The performance becomes about the singer's nerves instead of about the song. Knowing a story behind the song and having sensory cues gives you somewhere to go instead of focusing on how nervous you are. It helps you stay present so that your delivery is authentic, whether you have stage nerves or not.

For every song you perform, go through the same process of figuring out the mood, the sensory cues and the who-what-when-where-why. This enables you to know the song backwards and forwards, and to own it.

Chapter 8:
Focus

Now that you've analyzed what you want to accomplish as a performer, tweaked your vocal technique, and gotten a handle on the lyrics of your performance songs, you have a great foundation. It's time now to start some actual performance rehearsals (finally!). Your initial work will be in front of a mirror, preferably a good-sized one where you can see most of your body. The rehearsal exercises will be interspersed with role model study exercises. This is so you can analyze other performers to see what moves work for them, and to get additional movement and gesture ideas.

Doing the rehearsal exercises

Repeat each rehearsal exercise as many times as you need to until you feel a sense of mastery. Even if that means you stay with an exercise for several weeks, try to get comfortable with each new detail of your performance before moving onto the next exercise.

Please keep in mind that rules are meant to be broken. I can pretty much guarantee that as soon as I write "Don't point while singing," you'll see a great performance by someone who is pointing as they sing. The purpose of these rehearsal exercises is for you to become aware of and to stop anything you're doing that is weakening your performance, and then to grow comfortable with more effective movements. You'll be trying some different moves on for size and it may feel awkward at first, like you're trying to learn a new dance. Ideally, with enough practice all these movements will feel like a natural extension of the mood and meaning of the song.

Direct Eye Focus

Standing in front of the mirror, look yourself in the eye and sing your entire song, without losing eye contact.

Some singers find this exercise very easy to do, but many do not. You may discover at first that you look away dozens of times throughout the song. You may realize that you've been singing with your eyes closed most of the time and so keeping your eyes open feels unnatural.

If you accompany yourself you may realize that you've been looking at your fingers a great deal while singing. If you're an accomplished enough player you may discover that you no longer need to do this. Or you may find that you just need an occasional glance at your hands on the tricky parts. Put in the practice time to free yourself from looking at your hands and your overall performance will improve dramatically.

I would discourage you from making direct eye contact with someone in the audience while performing. Not only is it a bit much for them to handle, but it can distract you and disrupt your concentration. Instead, learn to focus on foreheads. This gives the illusion of eye contact but is less confrontational. Try it when talking to a friend and ask if they can tell that you aren't looking them in the eye. Whenever I talk about making eye contact in this book I will be referring to this kind of eye contact. Though there will be times when you should make an exception to this rule, train yourself so eye-to-forehead contact is your default mode.

Forehead Eye Focus

Sing your song into the mirror again, this time focusing on your forehead. Maintain your focus for the entire song.

This will probably be much easier than the previous exercise. If so, try to concentrate on the lyric as you maintain eye-to-forehead contact.

What *not* to do with your eyes while performing

I'm sure you've seen many famous performers singing with their eyes squeezed shut for the entire song. Did you think that having their eyes closed improved the performance? In general, I'm against it since it shuts the audience out. Closing your eyes for a dramatic moment or to concentrate during a difficult or emotional passage is fine. Then open your eyes again. I can't tell you how many singers have seduced me on the radio or on CD, only to lose me when I saw them perform with their eyes shut for most of the song. Eye contact is such a powerful way to communicate when performing, why would you ignore it?

Watch for the habit of looking down frequently as you perform. Your eyes will be open, but to your audience it will look like they are closed. Also watch for looking *above* heads in the audience unless you're singing an inspirational song. Another exception would be if you're performing in a venue with a balcony. That being said, most of the time when you are singing to an audience, look at foreheads.

The two eye contact exercises you just did serve several purposes:
1. If you haven't watched yourself sing in the mirror before they initiate you to that valuable process.
2. They help you hone the skill of maintaining focus while staying tuned in to the lyric.
3. If you look around too much as you sing (I call that "flitting"), they help you break that habit.

In real life performing you will probably not want to focus on one forehead for an entire song. It looks unnatural, too theatrical and confrontational. (Of course, if you're singing a confrontational song you can use that!) Most of the time you won't want to be fixed on one point. Nor would you want to start looking everywhere. That's flitting, which comes across as nervous and spacey. One way to look focused without being fixed on one spot is to use a "movable focus."

Movable Focus

Face a wall of your practice room and pick at least three points on the wall approximately at eye level. You can use posters on the wall, coffee cups, whatever. Or you can put post-its on the wall to represent audience members.

Sing the first phrase or two of your song to one of your focal points. (A phrase is like a musical sentence, usually punctuated with a breath.) Then sing the next phrase or two to another focal point. Continue singing the entire song, switching your focus every phrase or two.

Who are you singing this lyric to? That's where your lyric study comes in. Let's suppose you are singing to your best friend. Sing the song again, using the same movable focus, but this time imagine that your best friend is moving around the room so that you are still singing to him or her even as your focus shifts.

Using a movable focus can be a very effective way to communicate to an audience. You want to include the entire audience without losing your concentration, and a movable focus allows you to do that.

There are many ways to use one's eyes besides what you did in these last three exercises. How do you know what kind of focus is right for you? Let's revisit your list of role models and see what works for them.

While you will learn something from watching good artists who are outside your chosen genre, you'll have a better chance of learning what is appropriate for your style from role models who are doing something closer to what you're doing. Youtube has tons of videos of live performances, and you can also rent concert DVDs (or get them from the library). Performances from regular music videos can be useful, but keep in mind that most are highly edited. You'll get a better sense of an actual

performance from videos of live performances. Look at the following
questions before you watch each video so you know what to study. Of
course you can see live performances, too!

Focus Research

Watch at least four performances by artists on your list of
role models. After watching each performance jot down
some answers.

Artist Name: _____
Song Title: _____

1. Was this a strong performance?
2. If no, why not? (You can learn just as much from a bad
performance as you can from a good one)

3. If yes, what was the artist's focus like: Steady? Eyes
closed? Flitting? Movable focus? Something else?

4. If the artist maintained steady or movable eye focus did
they appear to be singing to another person (as opposed to
an inanimate object)?

5. If not, what were they singing to? The ceiling, the floor,
heaven? Was this effective?

6. Did the performer come across as natural? Stiff? Overly
theatrical?

7. Is this performance a good example of an effective use
of focus?

8. Write down anything else noteworthy about the
performer's focus.

If you answered "Yes" to question #7, study the performance more deeply: does the artist occasionally look to the side as if they were thinking or flirting? Susannah Hoffs of the Bangles did this to good effect in several videos including "Walk Like an Egyptian." Do they maintain steady eye focus but break it up by looking at the floor occasionally to make it more natural looking? Jennifer Nettles of Sugarland does this in their video for "Stay."

Think about the lyric of your song again and recall the word cues you created during your lyric study. For this next exercise, connect what you are saying in the lyric with what feels like the right focus. Ideally, your focus will flow organically from what you're singing and will both feel and look natural, but it could take a fair amount of rehearsal to get to that point.

If there was anything that you saw one of your role models do with their eyes that you want to try as you sing your song, now's your chance.

One More Time with Focus

Go back to the mirror and sing your song, staying aware of your lyric cues and using your best judgment of what is an appropriate amount of steady and movable focus. You can also try occasionally closing your eyes, looking down, or looking away if it feels right. Try adding something you saw one of your role models do with their eyes.

Chapter 9:
The Rest of Your Face & Head

Where you focus your eyes is a vital part of your performance, but the rest of your face communicates a great deal, too. While doing your focus research you probably noticed some facial movements your role models made that helped or hindered their performances. Let's discuss some of these now.

Eyebrows

I saw a lifeless performance years ago and couldn't put my finger on what was wrong, since the performer's songs and vocals were great. I finally realized that the artist never moved his eyebrows once the entire show. Though he was engaged in what he was doing, it wasn't coming across to the audience. Instead, he looked numb. Some great performers like James Taylor, Marvin Gaye, Justin Timberlake and Ronnie Dunn know the value of active eyebrows. By active I mean up and down movement. Of course you can overdo this and look psychotic, but occasional gentle lifts of the eyebrows can communicate a lot. And from a vocal technique standpoint, a gentle lift of the eyebrows can help open your voice so it isn't stuck in your throat.

What I call a 'crunch' is when you squeeze your eyebrows together like you're worried. It's very common for artists to crunch on high notes, and some singers will crunch for an entire song. The problem is that crunching makes you look severe and worried, probably not what you're trying to communicate. Also, tension between the eyes often goes hand in hand with throat tension, which will adversely affect your singing. I would say that unless you are singing punk, crunching is something you should only do occasionally if the lyric calls for it. Many singers have a habit of crunching a lot and don't ever realize it until they sing into the mirror. Sometimes just becoming aware of it can help you correct the habit. If you need more help than that, one trick is to put some tape between your eyes when you practice so you can feel every time you squeeze your brows together. The best thing to do if you don't want to crunch is to lift your brows instead.

Eyes

There's another eye movement I haven't mentioned yet and the only way to detect it is either to videotape yourself or have a friend tell you. Sometimes a singer will halfway close their eyes during a passionate phrase. The singer thinks that her eyes are shut since all she sees is black, but the audience sees half-shut eyelids and the whites of the singers eyes. Very unflattering! Make sure if you close your eyes when singing that you close them all the way.

Mouth

How much or how little you open your mouth and what looks good will vary from style to style: singers who belt usually open wide to wail those high notes. This includes many rock, soul, punk, and blues singers. Musical theater singers use their mouths a great deal to hyper-articulate each word. Folk, bluegrass and many country singers often only open a bit more than they do when speaking. Since there is a wide range of what singers do, you'll need to study other singers, study yourself and make your own decision as to what looks right. Voice technique-wise, in general, you shouldn't over-open your mouth more than two finger-widths, or like you're eating a thick sandwich. Repeated hyper-extension of the jaw can lead to jaw problems. You need to use your mouth more when singing than when you're speaking, just be wary of going to extremes (unless you are an extreme kind of performer). You also don't want to keep your mouth too closed, which can look tense and restrict your sound.

Watch for too much smiling when singing, or what I call 'pulling'. A slight smile while singing is fine, but sometimes when singers reach a difficult high note they suddenly pull their mouths into an unflattering extreme smile. It looks and works better to drop the jaw instead. Some singers, like Stevie Wonder, smile a lot while they sing and make it work, so it's not out of the question. Just make sure if you choose to smile a lot while singing that it looks natural and not forced.

Another thing to watch for is jaw wobble. That's when a singer is gliding over several notes on one vowel sound and the mouth wobbles with each note change. This can look pretty weird. Most singers can correct it by spending some time singing into the mirror.

The mouth can do all kinds of other subtle moves: watch Elvis Presley footage to see how he curled his upper lip, then watch Sheryl Crow to see how she curls her upper lip in a different but also very effective way. Aretha Franklin closes her mouth in-between phrases in a way that exudes confidence. Jennifer Nettles conveys a lot of emotion by using her mouth much more than many other female country singers. Prince sometimes smiles briefly while singing in a wonderfully suggestive way.

Making Faces

Some great singers, like Joe Cocker, make lots of faces while singing. Other equally great singers, like Alison Krauss, look like they are barely working to produce a beautiful sound. There is a huge range of what's acceptable as a performer. Ultimately it's your choice: if you are a passionate performer who thinks that lots of face movement frees up your sound and helps you sing and communicate better then go with that, but videotape yourself at some point so you are aware of the face you're presenting to the world.

Head

Most of the time, try to keep your head in a neutral position so your nose is pointed straight ahead, neither up nor down. It's less common to see a performer tilt their head down while singing, but many singers tilt their heads up too much or jut out their chins. This angle can put some strain on your vocal cords. Technically and visually, a neutral position with your head neither up nor down is better. As I mentioned in the *Focus* chapter, the exception is if you have a balcony of people to include.

If your head is fixed in one position for the entire song you'll look like a robot. You need some movement to look natural. But just as it looks weird when your eyes are darting around, it also looks odd when your head is moving around too much. During a beat-heavy song your head may move with the beat of the music in-between phrases, but when singing that should ease up. Side-to-side head movement (as if you are slowly shaking your head "no") is fine and can help you include the entire audience. Since your head will usually follow what your eyes are doing, keep employing a movable focus. That will help keep your head movements looking natural.

There are all kinds of exceptions to this rule. Singer/players in bands will look at their instruments and each other a lot during the course of a song. I've also seen singers move their heads a lot while performing and not look jerky or unfocused. But as a general guideline, watch for frenetic head movement or keeping your head locked in one place. You would think that singing into mic that's on a stand would restrict movement a bit, but I've seen singers move their heads all over the place even when on mic.

One thing I've often noticed with singers who move their heads too much is that the rest of their bodies are barely moving. It's like they are channeling all of their energy and expression into their heads. Once they learn to move their bodies a bit more the relentless head movement calms down.

Review of face and head movements

- **Eyebrows:** use them for enhanced expressiveness, but don't crunch too much. Try lifting them instead.
- **Eyes:** close them all the way if you close them.
- **Mouth:** don't under- or over-open it, do what seems right for your style, and watch out for pulling.
- **Head:** keep it in a neutral position, tilted neither up nor down. Watch for too much or too little movement.

Remember, what works for one style of music might look forced in another. That's where your role model viewing comes in.

Face & Head Research

Watch a minimum of four performances (total, not each) by your role models. Find performances that include a lot of close-up shots. After each viewing answer the following questions:

1. Was this an effective performance?
2. If not, why not?

a. Was it bad vocal technique (singing out of tune, strained tone, mumbling)?

b. Was it lack of focus or funny facial or head movements?

3. Were their eyes open, closed, or a combination?

4. Where was their focus? How often did it shift?

5. Did they use their eyebrows to communicate? If so, how much and how often?

6. How much did they open their mouth?

7. How much and how often did they smile, if at all?

8. How much and how often did they move their head?

9. Was their head tilted up, down, or in a neutral position?

I'm sure you get the idea here. I want you to pick apart the facial and head movements of several of your role models so you have an idea of what is appropriate for your musical style. You might also find some moves that you'll want to try when you rehearse.

Face & Head Rehearsal

Face the mirror and sing your song, taking note of your eyes, eyebrows, mouth and head position. It may be difficult to focus on *what* you're saying as you do this, but try to sing with some feeling so that you do the movements you usually do when singing. Watch in particular for crunching, not opening your mouth enough, tilting your head up and/or moving your head around too much since these are the most common problems singers have. If you notice any problems, correct them one at a time— it can drive you crazy trying to fix everything at once. Remember that most of these facial corrections can result in it feeling easier to sing.

Be patient with yourself if you need to correct a bad habit or two. If you've been crunching for years you won't be able to fix it in one session. Give yourself time to replace any bad habits with good ones.

A quick aside on technique: if you are seeing signs of strain in your throat such as bulging veins, you may need to readdress your voice technique. Keep in mind that some throats reveal more than others. If you are very thin you may see movement in your throat that doesn't necessarily indicate tension. If you are plumper your throat may show nothing visually, but you may still be tensing it when singing. If you both *see* and *feel* strain, then you definitely have some technique work to do.

Face & Head Rehearsal with Lyric Focus

When you feel that your face and head look good as you sing, quickly review the back-story, mood, imagery and tactile cues for your song. Sing your song again, focusing this time on really delivering the lyric, and notice if your face and head movements change at all. Also notice if your face and head movements work with the mood and story you are delivering. You wouldn't want to smile throughout a bitter song, nor would you want to crunch your eyebrows and look worried during a hopeful song. Make adjustments. This is a good time to borrow some of the moves you saw your role models make and try them on for size.

You will probably find that you lose your focus on the lyric as you experiment and make any visual adjustments. Don't worry about it, just get back to the lyric after each adjustment. One of my worst gigs ever was at a club where the stage faced a bar with a huge mirror behind it. I kept watching myself instead of focusing on the lyric and connecting with the audience.

During many of these exercises you may find yourself being overly focused on your physical movements. That's fine, but your ultimate goal is to have rehearsed them enough that they become a natural extension of the lyric.

Chapter 10:
Arms & Hands

Watch people as they are talking and you'll often see all kinds of hand movements as they tell you about their bad day at work or their great date the night before. The speakers won't be thinking about what their hands are doing, but their hands will help them express themselves. Now watch several performers who aren't playing instruments and you'll also see lots of hand movements. Some will look natural, but some will look stagey and forced. Figuring out what to do with one's hands is a problem for many singers. Some hold onto the mic for dear life, some resort to theatrical moves, some just give up and put their hands in their pockets. Your goal in this chapter is to find some hand movements that feel and look natural, are appropriate for your style of music, and help you express the lyric of your song.

What is successful here is very subjective. One performer can throw her hand to the sky and make it work, the next one looks like a tacky Vegas lounge singer. Gospel and pop/R&B singers use arm movements a lot, and often will dance their hands along with their elaborate vocal runs. If a bluegrass singer did that it would look strange. Different musical styles inspire different hand and arm movements.

If you play an instrument and sing you may not be worried about hand and arm movements, but read this chapter anyway since you may periodically raise your arm from the guitar or keyboard to gesture.

Some tips about hand and arm movements

1. Don't clamp your hands to your thighs because you don't know what to do with your hands. It looks unnatural. Even a tender ballad needs more movement than that.

2. Don't point. I rarely see someone point while singing and not look fake. Look at politicians making speeches: they all emphasize what they are saying with closed fists or open flat hands. The pollsters figured out long ago that audiences don't

respond well to pointing. While singing, a flat open hand will look more natural and relaxed than a clenched fist.

3. Use hand movements you might use when talking. Most of us use our hands when talking in subtle ways. Incorporate these moves for your performances. If you don't ever use your hands when talking then watch friends talking and use their gestures.

4. Feel the beat. Occasionally tapping your thigh along with the beat of the song can add energy. (Don't do this if you can't keep a beat, however!) Finger snapping looks dated, so I would stick to thigh tapping.

5. Let your hands follow the lyric— that's your best bet for having natural movements. However...

6. Watch out for acting out the lyric too literally. Pointing at your cheeks when you sing about crying, waving bye-bye while singing "Goodbye, baby," or chugging an imaginary shot while singing a drinking song can come across as very cheesy.

Hand & Arm Movement Research

Let's see what the experts can show you about good hand and arm movement. Watch at least four performances, this time making sure that there are fewer close-up and more full or half-body shots to watch. Make some quick decisions about whether you like or dislike what the performer does with her hands, and then spend some time only watching the performers who have hand and arm movements you like. Answer these questions about each performance:

1. Did the performer move her hands a lot, a bit, or hardly at all? If hardly at all, where did her hands rest?

2. What were her hand positions— open, close-fisted, pointing, or what? Did she change her hand positions a lot or rarely?

3. If both of her hands were free did she move them at the same time, or did one of her hands do most of the gesturing?

4. Did her hand and arm movements seem spontaneous or rehearsed?

5. Did they bring out the feeling of the song?

6. Did her hands move independently of the beat, with it, or a combination?

Take note of any gestures that you can try adding to your performance.

Copping moves from other performers is fine— they probably stole them from someone else. Don't steal obvious moves, however, like Elvis Presley's distinctive hip swivel or James Brown's schtick with the cape. An obvious steal will make you look like a goofball, but if someone lifts their hand or stomps their foot a certain way that looks good, go ahead and try adding it to your performance. Of course you will need to practice it for awhile *and* make sure that it works with what you are trying to communicate or it will look contrived or out of place.

Hand & Arm Movement
Rehearsal Part 1

Now it's time to see how your gestures are helping or hindering your own performance. Sing your song into the mirror and observe what your hands do. Do this even if you often perform with an instrument or a hand-held mic. Getting comfortable performing with both hands free will build your confidence. If you like what you see then you're good to go. However, if like many performers, you suddenly feel stiff and awkward, just wave your hands around to loosen up. Do some overly theatrical moves as you sing that you are sure you'll never do for an audience. Then try some of the moves you saw your role models do or that you've seen your friends do while talking. Some great singers feel so stiff when it comes to arm and hand movements that the only thing that works for them is to find a few gestures that work and rehearse them until they become second nature. Try raising one hand, then both hands. Try clasping them together. Try tapping your thigh or your heart. Try moving your hand or hands without moving your arms. Experiment and play until you find some moves that work for you.

Hand & Arm Movement Rehearsal Part 2

If your movements continued to feel contrived during the last exercise, try this one: Stand with your arms relaxed at your sides. Close your eyes and *recite* the words to your song. Feel the lyric and allow your hands and arms to move naturally, as if you were telling a story to a friend. Don't think too much about what you're doing, just let the movements come naturally. Next, *sing* your song, still with your eyes closed, and let your arms and hands do similar movements. You're letting the lyric tell your hands what to do. Then sing your song again, this time watching yourself in the mirror, to see if these movements that stemmed organically from the lyric look natural to you.

It can take a long time to develop natural hand movements. Continue watching and analyzing other performers and continue to let the song tell your hands where to go.

Chapter 11:
Hips, Legs & Feet

Some singers use only the upper half of their body to deliver the song. But even if you are playing an instrument while singing you can move the lower half of your body. Using your entire body to express yourself can add depth and power to your performance.

How much to move

What kind of performer are you? Do you tend to sing subtle ballads or are you a high-energy rock & roller? How much or how little you move the rest of your body when performing is directly affected by your performing goals, persona and intention. If you sing thoughtful folk songs that send your audience into a quiet reverie you may not move much at all. If your intention is to have your audience on their feet, clapping and dancing, you will be using your body a lot to build that kind of energy. There's a wide range of moves you can make in-between those two extremes. If you need to, review your answers to your persona and intention exercises, or review the first daydreaming exercise and notice if your body moved a lot or a little during your performance. Keep in mind that movement from the waist down is more earthy and nonintellectual. Use gentle moves to add a touch of sexiness to your performance, or use big moves to connect with your audience in a more primal way.

Let's look at two categories of movement. The first are those that you can do if you're singing into a mic that's on a stand. The second kind you can make if you are singing without a mic or are hand-holding a mic.

Singing with a mic and stand

Some performers dread the idea of hand-holding the mic while moving during a performance for fear of looking like a lounge singer— they'd rather work with a stand mic. Obviously you can't run around the stage; you're rooted in one place and your mouth can't stray far from the mic if you want to be heard. (By the way, there's a chapter up ahead on mic technique.) However, both of your hands are free, and there's a lot you can do from the waist down. For example:

- **Hips***:* Whether a very subtle sway or an earthy bump and grind, whether side to side or back and forth, a rhythmic hip sway can be very sexy. Hip movements can also relax your torso, making it easier to breathe and therefore easier to sing. I would highly recommend that you work out a rhythmic hip sway that is comfortable for you unless it's really inappropriate for your musical style. At some point you'll want to have an easy movement that you can fall into without thinking. It can make you look relaxed even when you're nervous. You can practice swaying anytime you're standing and listening to music with a beat. If hip swaying just isn't your style, try just shifting your weight from one foot to another. Make sure you're moving with the beat.

- **Feet***:* Though one of my college music professors admonished us to never tap our feet, you'll see it all over the place in contemporary music. Again, make sure that you're tapping with the beat— it's very disconcerting to the audience if you are singing a song in one tempo and tapping your foot in another! If you're in a small venue or at an audition don't tap so loudly that it can be heard unless you are deliberately adding audible foot percussion. Sometimes your entire leg starts moving along with your foot tap. This can be very dramatic and can work really well on beat-heavy songs. Avoid this in ballads, please!

- **Choreographed moves***:* it's beyond the scope of this book to dive deeply into the world of dance, but if you plan to add choreographed dance moves to your act, work with a capable choreographer. Bad choreography can turn an okay performer into something laughable, but good choreography and execution can make you a star. Look at what it did for Michael Jackson and Justin Timberlake. Use several full-length mirrors in your rehearsal space, and make good use of a video camera.

If you have problems keeping a consistent beat, if you have problems with moving your hips and/or legs, or if you just feel unsure about what to do with your body, do what I did years ago and take a dance class. I had no ambition whatsoever to be a dancer, I just wanted to feel more comfortable on stage and it helped a lot.

If you play an instrument while you sing you'll need to find moves that don't mess up your playing. Or, only do them during the less demanding sections of a song. If you've been sitting or standing still while playing and singing and you realize that adding some movement will help your presentation, give yourself time to get used to the added movement. Don't throw out your great guitar technique just to add some fancy footwork, but if you aren't already, start practicing your instrument standing up (if possible) while gradually adding some hip, leg or feet moves.

Some movements *not* to do

- **Wiggling:** Some performers are so happy to be singing that it comes out in a joyous wiggle. Try replacing it with some kind of slower movement, like a sway. Charo is a performer who can get away with wiggling, but on everyone else it looks funny.

- **Double-time movement:** This is when your hips move twice as fast as they should. You're moving with the beat but it looks frenetic. For example, imagine the Beatle's song "Come Together." If you tap your hand or foot eight times during the first phrase "Here come old flattop, he come-" then you're counting in double-time. That won't look too odd, but if your hips and/or shoulders are swaying back and forth that quickly it'll look pretty weird. If you're doing a steady movement like that, try doing it half as fast.

Singing without a mic, or with a hand-held mic or headset

Some performers just love the freedom and power of being able to work the entire stage. When you have the whole stage to use, your choice of movement opens up considerably. Whether pacing, dancing, or running, you have more range of movement and more room to do it in. This can add loads of energy to your performance: think of how Garth Brooks galvanized country music by adding rock show high-energy moves to his live performances. These days we see more and more headsets on singers at bigger shows. These free up the entire body. Again, the style of music you are doing and whether you are playing an instrument will influence whether you go hand-held mic or not (if you are on mic, that is). Another thing that will influence you is the type of performance you are doing and the size of the venue. At most auditions you probably won't be racing around the room or stage as you sing. By and large your auditioners want to see how you sing as if you are at a mic and stand. Nor would you probably climb on the speakers at a coffee shop or other small venue show. It can look pretentious when you do stadium-sized moves in a 70-seat room. At bigger shows you can go for bigger moves.

Some movements to try

Move in-between phrases: If you watch singers who are also dancing or otherwise covering some ground, you'll notice that they will often strike a pose to sing a phrase. Then they'll move some more before they strike another pose while they sing the next phrase. It's hard to maintain good breath support to sing while moving energetically. That's why many dancer-singers lip-sync their songs when performing live. If most of your big moves are in-between phrases you'll have better control of your singing. A variation on the pose-striking technique is to simply tone down your movements while singing. An easy walk won't mess with your breathing like a bunch of fancy footsteps.

Movable focus: Remember when I discouraged letting your eyes dart around while singing since it looks crazy and unfocused? Moving around while singing can have the same effect if you don't maintain your focus. If you use a movable focal point you can work the stage and still come across as focused and in control. Remember to whom you are singing the song and direct your song to that person even if you are running across the stage. Your movable focus can move with you.

Moving with or without the beat: You can make every move in time with the rhythm, ignore the beat, or do a combination of both. Moving without the beat looks more casual, while moving with the beat emphasizes the rhythm and gets the audience feeling it more. The only thing I *wouldn't* do is move rhythmically in a different tempo than the song tempo. You'll just look like you have no sense of rhythm at all.

Get in shape: If you do plan to have a very physical act including loads of movement, you'll need to be in great shape. Make sure lots of aerobic exercise like running or dancing is part of your regimen.

Finding moves that work for you whether you are in a fixed position or not will involve a fair amount of experimentation. Try these next three exercises to help you develop your own moves.

Waist & On Down Research

Watch at least four performances that involve hip, leg and/or foot movement. Cameras often show only from the waist up, so you may need to search a bit. If you can't find this kind of performance from any of your role models, find performers outside your musical genre and study them. Here are some questions to ask yourself about their movements:

1. Do they look natural or forced?

2. Do they add to the performance or are they distracting?

3. Are they fun to watch?

4. Are they rhythmic, have no set beat, or are they a combination of both?

5. Do they seem choreographed or improvised?

6. Are there any moves you could incorporate?

Waist & On Down Rehearsal Without Singing

This exercise is valuable even if you tend to sing a lot of

ballads, and can be done while staying in one place or moving about the room. There are many singers who have yet to develop a good sense of rhythm and are terrified that someone will find out. If you are one of them you'll need privacy for this exercise, so lock the door! Play the track for your song. If you don't have one because you accompany yourself, play a recording of yourself singing the song. Dance to your song. This can be a minimalist dance or a major Gene Kelly epic. Just let your body find the song's groove and move with it in some fashion. If you notice that all of your movements are in your arms and head, try moving your lower half a bit too, even if it's just to tap your feet. Try any of the moves you saw during your research. Stay away from the mirror at first. If you find a move that you like, eventually check it in the mirror to see if it looks as good as it feels.

Waist & On Down Rehearsal With Singing

Step away from the mirror, play the music track for your song and sing with it, moving at the same time. Try to connect with the lyric as you sing so that the lyric informs your moves, and let your body fall into some of the moves you did in the previous exercise. Keep experimenting until you find some moves that feel like a logical extension of the lyric. Then get back in front of the mirror to check them out. If you're working on non-stationary moves you'll be moving in and out of what you can see in the mirror. Do the best you can and check them out more fully when you can record your performance on video.

Chapter 12:
Posture

Your posture communicates a great deal to your audience long before you've opened your mouth. Slumping makes you look like a follower, while good posture makes you look like a leader. I worked with a handsome singer a few years ago who had a wonderful, rich, soulful voice. Viewed from the front his posture seemed fine, but in profile his head jutted forward so much that he looked like he was overly straining. It really detracted from his looks and from the warmth of his performance, so we did a lot of work to correct his posture. This included singing while lying on the floor and singing with his back pressed against a wall.

An off-balance relaxed stance, where you shift all of your weight to one leg and slouch a bit, can convey a casual feel that works well in some styles like rap and R&B. Take it farther and you'll look like you don't care a bit what anyone thinks. Make sure that's your intention if that's the posture you choose.

The other extreme is an overly erect stance, standing up hyper-straight with your shoulders and head pulled back. This is too rigid and military a posture and could tighten your throat, restrict your singing *and* make your audience uncomfortable.

Posture Exercise

1. Stand in front of a full-length mirror and close your eyes.

2. Hold your head in a neutral position, with your nose pointing straight ahead, not up or down. Imagine a string is extending from the crown of your head to the ceiling.

3. Now imagine the string is pulled taut. Your neck will

elongate and your chin won't be able to jut forward. Your rib cage should be up but not overly raised, your shoulders should be relaxed and down, not scrunched up, pulled back or curled forward. Your pelvis shouldn't tip forward too much or be tipped back, sticking your butt out too far.

4. When your posture feels right, open your eyes and see how you look in the mirror. Turn sideways to check as well. To get a good view of your profile, you may want to do this exercise again later in a dressing room with double mirrors or on camera.

If you find that you can't stop lifting your chin or overly bobbing your head around as you sing, balance an aluminum pie plate upside-down on your head as you sing a song. You'll get tired of leaning over to pick up the plate each time it falls off your head and eventually learn how to keep your head in a neutral position while singing.

Chapter 13:
Putting It All Together

At this point you've spent a lot of time isolating different parts of your body to develop movements that help you communicate your song. Ideally, as you shifted your focus from head to arm to hip movements you retained what you had already worked on. If that's the case, putting all of these moves together won't be too difficult. It bears repeating that all of your movements should be a natural extension of the lyric.

Putting it All Together Rehearsal

Review the back-story, overall mood, and any sensory cues for your song. Step away from the mirror and choose a wall to be your audience. Sing your song to the wall audience, feeling the lyric and letting your body fall into all of the movements you rehearsed in previous exercises. If you find yourself getting self-conscious about what an arm or foot is doing let your focus come back to the lyric and to whom you are singing the song.

Now get in front of the mirror again and step back enough so that you can see all or most of your body. Sing your song again with feeling and watch yourself in the mirror. It might be difficult to stay with the feeling as you watch yourself sing. You might want to make some visual adjustments and then move away from the mirror to sing your song again to the wall. You can continue alternating performances to the wall/audience and then to the mirror to see how you look. Every time you go back to singing to the wall get back to the meaning of the lyric.

If you have been working with more than one song, alternate between them. This way you have to approach each song fresh and quickly find the mood, meaning and moves for each one.

The next step is to test your performance further by videotaping yourself or singing for other people. But before you take that leap there are two topics I want to cover: mental attitude and stage nerves. If you aren't going to videotape yourself and plan on moving directly to doing live performances, first use the checklist in Chapter 16, *Videotaping Yourself*, to evaluate your performance in detail.

Chapter 14:
Mental Attitude

What does your attitude have to do with whether you give a great performance or not? Pretty much everything. Rehearsals, knowing voice technique, knowing your intention and persona, knowing your song inside out— all of these things build confidence and a good attitude. Confidence helps you to focus and perform better. But a bad attitude can distract and weaken you and bring your performance down, even with all the rehearsal in the world.

What do I mean by a bad attitude? I mean dwelling on negative thoughts like "I'll never be as good as..." or "I should be a much better singer by my age" or "I screwed up that last time, I bet I'll screw up again this time." We're all human and we all have thoughts like these, the choice is whether or not you let these thoughts sabotage your performance. They are just thoughts, they aren't *you*.

Building a positive attitude

If you study sports psychology and performance psychology you'll find that they are very similar. You'll also find that a positive attitude isn't necessarily something you are born with, or that you have only if you've had a happy childhood. It can be learned. A positive attitude doesn't mean that you never have negative thoughts; it means that you simply acknowledge them and replace them with positive thoughts. The ability to do this is something you can train into yourself. Then you must apply the technique during rehearsals and performances. Performing can be such a stressful endeavor that you need all of the mental tools you can muster to combat the nerves and distractions that can disrupt a performance. Learning to have a good attitude as a singer is one of these tools, and the time to acquire that ability is now.

There is an entire industry built around how to foster a good attitude and fight negative thoughts. Many books have been written on the subject, but my favorite is "Power Performance for Singers" by Alma Thomas and Shirlee Emmons. It goes much more deeply into this topic and I highly recommend it. It's geared towards classical singers, but most of the information is also applicable to contemporary vocal styles.

Here are some examples of negative thoughts followed by positive thoughts to replace them:

1. My voice is too thin. *When I practice a lot my voice sounds really good. My mother loves my voice.*
2. My arms always look stiff when I sing. *Lots of great performers were stiff at first. I know if I rehearse enough I'll relax.*
3. Why should I bother? There are so many other singers better than me. *Britney Spears, Neil Young, André 3000 and Bette Midler all have had great careers. They aren't the best singers around, but tons of people love them.*
4. I always strain for the high notes in that chorus. *When I warm up, relax, and breathe I can sing really high.*
5. I'm too old to be a good singer. *Tony Bennett is still singing and performing great and he's in his 80s.*

Replacing Negative Thoughts

Jot down four negative thoughts you've had about yourself as a singer or performer. Then come up with a positive counter-statement for each one.

1. Negative:
Positive:

2. Negative:
Positive:

3. Negative:
Positive:

4. Negative:
Positive:

Anytime negative thoughts arise when you are rehearsing, try replacing them with positive ones and see how it affects your performance. That doesn't mean that you shouldn't take note of problems that need correcting. If you noticed during the first focus exercise that you kept looking down while singing, that isn't a negative thought; that's awareness. But if you think "Wow, that's terrible, I'll never be a great performer if that's what I always do," then you've added a negative spin to your awareness of something that just needs to be corrected. Staying positive is a mental habit you can acquire that will help you immensely when the performance pressure is on.

The importance of a performance mantra

Remember when I asked you to create a few cue words for each song that would help you dive into the essence of the song? Now I want you to create some cue words about yourself as a performer. This mantra is something you can use when you are feeling distracted or stressed out before a performance. Of course, make sure that your mantra is a positive thought! Here are some ideas:

"When I sing I'm sending love out to the world."
"I'm the singer everyone has been waiting for."
"I'm an instrument of a higher power who takes over when I sing."
"I love to sing and the world loves to hear me."

You may think this sounds too new-agey, but when the pressure is on before a performance you will need somewhere for your mind to go. A mantra combined with deep breathing is a powerful relaxation tool. It can help you combat internal distractions like negative thoughts as well as external distractions like people chatting nearby when you're trying to get focused before a performance.

Creating & Using a Performance Mantra

Write your mantra here:

Lie down or sit in a comfortable chair and take some slow deep breaths. Count to five on each inhalation and each exhalation to slow and deepen your breaths. Now think your mantra on each inhalation and exhalation. Even doing this for only a minute can calm and focus you.

A variation on this is to inhale while thinking the things you want for your performance, then exhale while thinking the things you don't want. For example: "I breathe in confidence and focus, I breathe out my nervousness."

Try doing this exercise before each practice session, or in the middle of a rehearsal if you hit a mental or vocal block. Note how long it takes for you to relax. In the future you'll want to know how much time to set aside to reach a relaxed state.

During a performance you can't stop to lie down and take deep breaths if you are suddenly distracted by negative thoughts or external annoyances like too-bright lights, bad sound systems or noisy audiences. When that happens, briefly acknowledge the thought or distraction, then dive back into the song. Thinking a trigger thought like "Focus," "What am I saying right now?," or just "Right now!" can be enough to help you refocus. Don't try to fight the negative thought or distraction or it can overwhelm you. Take note of it, then move on.

These exercises can help you transcend disruptive performance stress, and can build the positive mental attitude that fuels a fantastic performance.

Singing Live

Chapter 15:
Handling Stage Fright

Nerves, stage fright, flutters...whatever you want to call it, it's the panic that hits many people facing a performance. Though stage fright can hit even the most seasoned performer, it does get better for most of us with experience.

One of the best ways to combat nerves is preparation. I don't think you can over-rehearse before a performance. All of the exercises and research you've done so far are part of that preparation, and preparation builds confidence. The more confident you feel about your performance, the less likely you are to suffer from debilitating butterflies.

You may also find that the more performances closer together you do, the easier it gets. If that's the case for you, you'll want to schedule several casual performances at open mics, karaoke bars, coffeehouses, etc. before an important gig. Several musical theater actor-singers I coached in LA made a practice of going to auditions they knew they weren't right for, simply to refine their auditioning chops and get used to performing under pressure.

If you haven't done a lot of performing and the idea of singing in public is truly terrifying, I recommend a step-by-step process, similar to gradually walking into a cold body of water. I'll outline this process later, after I go over some tips for working with nerves.

 Whether you are a newer or more experienced performer, if you've been working through this book and have done all of the exercises, you are now at a point where your singing and your performance should look and feel fairly polished. If not, go back and rehearse some more. Don't set yourself up for a bad initial performance experience by plowing ahead until you feel good about how you look and sound.

There are many things that you can do while still rehearsing on your own that will help you cope better when there are actual people watching you. Since stage fright is such a big issue for so many performers, I would try all of these methods to see which ones are the most helpful. Add the ones that work to your pre-performance ritual.

Many studies have shown that athletes who mentally rehearse their track meet, ski run or whatever beforehand consistently do better at the actual event. It's the same with singers. One of the things that evoke panic is the strangeness of suddenly being in front of a bunch of people staring at you. Unless we're touring musicians or have a steady gig, it's just not a situation most of us experience frequently. However, you can mentally prepare for this.

Mental rehearsal is also a great technique if you have a cold or any vocal fatigue during the days before a performance. You can still rehearse and reinforce all aspects of your performance without singing out loud.

Mental Rehearsal

Lie down or sit comfortably and mentally repeat your performance mantra along with deep breathing. Or substitute the silent message "I'm inhaling calm and peace, I'm exhaling all stress" as you breathe. Do this as long as you need to until you feel relaxed. Then, if you know the venue where your performance is going to be, call it to your mind. Imagine what the room looks like from the stage. Use your imagination if you don't know what the venue will look like. Many auditions are in small rooms with three people staring at you. Cattle call auditions such as American Idol are often in big rooms with several other singers performing at the same time as you. Imagine as many people watching you as you think will be at your performance. Then mentally execute your entire performance from start to finish, imagining as much detail as you can. Make all of the moves you rehearsed, dive into the essence of the song, and see the audience watching you. Give a fantastic performance where everything goes perfectly and let the audience show their appreciation when you finish.

Rehearsal with an Imaginary Audience

Perform your song as you imagine an audience watching you. If this alone gives you flutters, imagine that the audience is made up of your biggest fans. If you want to push the envelope and test yourself a bit, imagine that there are some people in the audience who scare you, like A&R executives or other great singers.

If you conjure up some nervousness while doing this, notice how your body responds. Is it harder to breathe? Do your arms feel stiff? Do you forget words? If you can determine exactly what happens to you when nervousness strikes, you can rehearse that aspect more. I always try to summon some nervousness before a gig and then take careful note of any mistakes I make, because I know those could be trouble spots in actual performances. If you work everything thoroughly enough, even if you're nervous you'll go on autopilot and still do fine.

Mental rehearsal and rehearsing with an imaginary audience should be two of the staples of your performance preparation, but there are many other tricks you can try. Try all of these before rehearsing for your imaginary audience and see which one helps the most. Some singers prefer more active methods, while some prefer quieter centering methods. Some, like me, incorporate a little of both.

Several techniques for calming nerves

- **Pressure points:** A former student of mine swears that this technique alone cured his lifelong stage fright and allowed him finally to sing in public. Using the pads of your fingers tap the following points in your body about as hard as you'd knock on a door, but not so hard that it's painful. Breathe deeply as you tap each spot 10-15 times, then move on to the next location: 1) just below the center or "apple" of your cheek bones. 2) on the underside of your collarbone, about 3 inches on either side of your sternum and straight up from your nipples. 3) on your sides, under your armpits, where a bra would be if you wore a bra (use your imagination, guys!). The singers for whom this works usually feel a sense of relaxation within 30 seconds of the first taps.

- **Vigorous movement:** Some singers get so wound up by nervousness that they need to shake it off before a performance. I've been known to dash into a backstage bathroom and jump around in the stall just before a performance. Running in place works well, too. Basically, do anything that gets your blood pumping and your breathing deeper.

- An opera singer taught me a similar method that cured her nerves. Operating on the theory that when performing one's heart rate is elevated, she always got her heart rate up right before rehearsing. She'd do a bunch of jumping jacks and then practice an aria. Her body learned how to perform well when her heart was beating rapidly so that when her heart rate rose at a performance her body knew what to do.

- **Vigorous breathing:** Nerves can tighten the abdomen, causing your breaths to become shallow. Panting like a dog while rapidly pushing in with your abdomen, like a fast belly laugh, can relax you and get you breathing deeply again. I wouldn't overdo this method just before a performance, though, since a lot of extra air can dry your vocal cords.

- Speaking of laughing, I did a great performance once after having dinner with a very funny friend who had me laughing so hard I was in tears. That's a great way to relax pre-show! Consider watching a few minutes of a funny movie before you head out for the venue.

- **Stretching:** When you read the *Tips From the Pros* chapter you'll notice how many of them mention yoga as part of their pre-performance ritual. I'm in that camp, too. Yoga or other kinds of stretches can counter the tension that nerves can bring to the body. It can get you breathing deeper and help you feel centered and focused. Try some different yoga postures or other kinds of stretches to learn which ones work best for you and add them to your arsenal of tricks.

- **Using your mantra:** Your mantra and deep breathing can help to ease flutters. You can also try repeating a positive reinforcement statement that specifically addresses your nervousness, like: "Nerves are just energy that will fuel my performance and make it amazing."

In a later chapter I'll talk about the importance of coming up with fixed warm up, exercise, and diet plans for the day of a show. These, too, will help keep you calm.

Beta blockers and alcohol

You may have heard that some performers use beta blockers to handle stage fright. Beta blockers such as Inderol interfere with the adrenaline response that gives you stomach flutters and a rapid heartbeat when nerves strike. They don't affect your vocal cords, just the adrenaline surge. Every doctor I've consulted has told me that used infrequently, beta blockers are safe for the average person to use. Of course, if you want to try them you should consult with your doctor first. I've used them several times and while they do indeed calm the flutters, they aren't without a downside. I've forgotten lyrics and become depressed, sometimes dramatically so, after a show. And forget about getting that wonderful performance high if you use beta blockers. I'd recommend combating your nerves with other methods.

I'm also against drinking alcohol before singing since it screws up your judgment. You'll think you're doing really well when you aren't. Besides, alcohol dries out the throat. Save that glass of wine for after the show.

When your nerves take over while performing

Most performers find that their nervousness begins to ebb once they hit the stage, but that can take a song or two. If it strikes you when on stage, breathe! The nerves are just another distraction like we discussed in the previous chapter. Acknowledge them, then let them go. Let all that rehearsal you've been doing tell your body and voice what to do automatically, and immediately think of one of your positive reinforcement trigger words or lines, like "Focus," or "What am I saying right now?" This is to interrupt the flow of the nerves and help you focus on something else. All the prep work you did dissecting the lyric and mood of your song comes into play now. Instead of giving into the nervousness, dive into your song, and use all that adrenaline to fuel your performance. Keep breathing deeply!

If you are one of those performers who flush a bright red when adrenaline hits, one baby aspirin daily for several days prior to the performance will help.

Dealing with external distractions

Sometimes when nerves hit a singer becomes overly focused on external things, like how loud the drums are, or a grumpy looking audience member. You can't stop the thoughts that bombard you, but you can prevent them from taking over. Register them quickly and then get back to your song. As for audience members, I can't tell you how many times I thought someone out there was a hostile audience member, only to have them come up to me afterward to tell me how much they loved my show. They weren't grumpy— they were concentrating! If you find yourself dwelling on what different audience members might be thinking, either find a sympathetic person and focus on their forehead, or look in-between two people and focus there, imagining that whomever the lyric is directed towards is sitting there. And remember, most of people in the audience want you to do well— they're rooting for you!

The step-by-step desensitizing process

If you haven't performed much and have some big-time fear issues about performing for actual people, try a step-by-step desensitizing process. This process can be done before, after, or concurrently with any videotaping you want to do. If the idea of doing this is too much for you, move ahead to videotaping yourself, and try just imagining that someone you know is watching you as you perform. After you've done enough videotaping, come back to do this process.

Stay with each step until you are ready to do the next one. If you are someone with severe performance anxiety you will need to move very slowly, even waiting a week or more between each step. If this process is easy for you it's fine to move through all of the steps in one session.

Gradual Performances

Step One: Mentally choose your first listener. This should be a friend or loved one who is very supportive and wants to hear you sing. Without your listener present, rehearse your song while imagining that they are right in front of you listening. If butterflies hit you, use all of the techniques to ease nervousness outlined in this chapter.

Step Two: Your listener now joins the process. Tell them that you need to use them to work through your fears about singing and that they are not to give you any feedback. No helpful hints, no constructive criticism. All they are allowed to say after you sing is "That was nice, thanks."

Step Three: Set the scene. You're trying to create a very low-pressure performance environment. Your listener needs to be occupied with something so you don't think that 100% of their focus is upon you. They could be washing dishes, paying the bills, or doing a puzzle— something that doesn't involve talking. Spell out to them that you basically want them to ignore you, and then move to another room to sing.

Step Four: Keep singing and walk through the room where your listener is occupied. Stand behind them so there's no eye contact and keep singing.

Step Five: When you're ready, sit your listener in a chair and perform your song for them.

You can modify this process to suit your needs. Perhaps you'll sing for a friend as you're driving somewhere. Maybe your listener will sing *with* you the first time, which should really take the pressure off. Maybe you'll be in your room singing just knowing that your listener can remotely hear you through the walls.

After Step Five you can start thinking about singing for other people you know, joining a performance group, or hitting the karaoke clubs.

I invented my own process for conquering my terror. Halfway through college I started taking music classes despite my intense stage fright. I knew I'd be singing in class about eight weeks into the semester, so I had a limited time to work through my fears. I lived in a big house with six roommates, and I instructed all of them to ignore me when I sang. Whenever some of them were fixing dinner I'd grab my guitar and stroll through the kitchen, singing and playing.

My next step was a bit more radical. I got a gig singing and playing at a local restaurant. It was very low-pressure and low-profile, I just sat in the corner and played unamplified for tips and dinner. Everyone was busy eating and I was just background music. At least that's what I told myself, which got me through several weeks comfortably. Then one of the regulars shocked me by requesting that I play at her wedding. I had no idea anyone was listening that intently to me! Luckily by then I had grown more comfortable with performing.

Coping with severe performance anxiety

Some people have such severe performance anxiety that all of the methods outlined here, with the exception of beta blockers, simply won't do the trick. If this is the case with you, I'd recommend finding a good cognitive behavioral therapist to work with. Though many people find that addressing their issues with traditional therapy is useful for performance anxiety, CBT appears to be the therapy of choice these days. Studies have shown that in the long run, CBT is more effective than medication for easing severe performance anxiety.

Chapter 16:
Videotaping Yourself

If you own or have access to some kind of video recording device, you can use it to further refine your performance before presenting yourself to a real audience. This is a very effective way to scrutinize yourself and can really help you polish your act. As the saying goes, the camera doesn't lie. Be prepared— I was depressed for several days after seeing myself on video for the first time. I discovered that I'd been looking at the stage much of the time, which made it look like my eyes were closed.

How to best use videotaping to polish your performance

The camera will pick up little things you may have missed while singing into the mirror. Also keep in mind that the camera can't always capture the energy a performer generates in a room. I've been in the audience at several shows that I thought were fantastic, then saw them later on video and thought I was watching a different, less-inspired performance. Also, the sound quality on tape is often not great, so take note of what you hear, but don't take it as gospel. If you're out of tune, that's worth addressing, but if your tone quality is thin, record yourself on good quality audio equipment before you panic. Use videotaping primarily as a way to polish the visual aspects of your performance.

Videotaping Yourself

Play your backing track and sing your song at full performance level while taping yourself. It's fine if you want to focus directly on the camera or slightly above it, as if you were focusing on the camera's "forehead." But if you want the camera to film a typical performance to an audience of more than one person, use a movable focus.

If you're happy with your performance upon review, you can move on to the next exercise.

If videotaping yourself brings up some nervousness, review the last chapter or just breathe deeply and try again. Notice which part of your performance suffers when you get butterflies: your intonation, your arm movements, what? Whatever it is, practice it more. You don't need to watch what you've filmed until you think you've got a good take.

If you feel overwhelmed by videotaping and suspect that you've lost your grip on synchronizing singing, feeling the lyric, and physical movement, you can review the exercises in chapters 10 through 15 and film each one. In this way you'll be isolating and refining your different body movements, using the camera as a tool. Do this as long as necessary until you feel you've "put it all together" on film. Use this method too if you decide that you hate everything about your performance. In actuality you probably saw a couple of problems that were a nasty surprise and overreacted. Over time you will be able to view yourself more realistically.

Use the following visuals and vocals checklist to review what you've done. Having an itemized list can help you pinpoint problems in finer detail. Make lots of copies as you'll be using it frequently. The list starts with obvious physical moves and works its way towards more esoteric criteria like authenticity. Rate each item on a scale of 1 to 10 (10 being looks and/or sounds great), and if you like, add useful comments. Learn to work through the list quickly.

Evaluating Your Performance 1

Physical Movements	Rating	Comments
Focus:		
Eyes:		
Eyebrows:		
Mouth:		
Head Position:		
Head Stability:		
Arms and hands:		
Hips:		
Legs and feet:		
Choreography (Optional):		
Posture:		
Vocals		
Intonation & Accuracy:		
Tone quality:		
Diction & Articulation:		
Delivery:		
Phrase ends:		
Dynamics:		
Conveying the Lyric		
Emotional delivery:		
Pacing:		
Attitude:		
Authenticity:		

Use this next checklist to evaluate how you felt during your performance and if your performance matched up with your goals, persona and intention as a performer.

Evaluating Your Performance 2

Goals, Persona & Intention	Yes/No	Comments	
This performance:			
Was aligned with my performing goals:			
Conveyed my stage persona:			
Conveyed my performing intentions:			
Feelings While Performing			
I felt confident and in command:			
I felt nervous:			
If yes:			
Nerves eased up over time:			
Nerves didn't effect my performance:			
Other Comments			

Here are some explanations for the *Goals, Persona & Intention* questions:

This performance...
Was aligned with my performing goals: eg: if your goal is to be a huge rock star it was a huge rock performance.

Conveyed my stage persona: eg: if your stage persona is a sexy siren that's what you conveyed.

Conveyed my performing intentions: eg: if your intention is to make people cry it was a heart-wrenching performance.

If you record yourself to evaluate and polish your vocals you'll probably find that you work in finer and finer detail. It's the same with videotaping yourself. First focus on obvious problems like poor intonation, bad posture, or stiff hand gestures. Then hone finer details like articulation or emotional dynamics. Keep in mind that every aspect of your performance can influence other aspects. If you can't really get into the song emotionally, for example, your movements might be stiff. If your movements are too frenetic you'll be short of breath and your vocal tone and/or pitch may suffer.

Trust your gut when answering questions that are more subjective, like the quality of your emotional delivery. Remember what you learned from viewing your role models and use that as a guide.

One of the most important subjective questions is whether or not your performance feels and looks authentic. A thoroughly believable, commanding performance can transcend a lot of vocal and physical problems. The audience won't care if you hit a couple of flat notes or if you crunch your eyebrows too much if they are completely caught up in your performance. Keep polishing the details, but make sure to keep feeling and selling the song.

Chapter 17:
Audition Preparation

American Idol and similar open auditions

There are numerous national talent search shows that can provide wonderful career opportunities for singers. Many of them, like *American Idol*, are televised. This chapter addresses the specific needs you will have when preparing for one of these shows. Typically the first audition is a cattle-call, meaning you wait for hours, sometimes with hundreds of other singers, before you are heard. Then you sing a cappella (without accompaniment) for about 60 seconds for one of the production assistants. The evaluator may be writing notes on a clipboard throughout your performance. If you make it to the second round of auditions you may sing more of your song. You may be on mic, you may be filmed, and you may have a bigger audience. Because there are so many variables, the first thing to do is research the process as much as possible. Try to find out the full audition procedure and all of the requirements so that you can fully prepare in advance. Do you pick your audition song from a list the producers supply? Are you penalized if you sing for longer than 60 seconds? Will you be waiting inside or outside before the audition? Besides the official rules normally posted on the show's web site, there are often online blogs about the more popular auditions like *American Idol* where other singers post notes about their audition experiences.

As you learned earlier in this book, song selection is key. At an audition you have very little time to make an impact, so you want something that really shows you off. Assume that the people listening to you are tired, jaded and burnt out. They want to be completely knocked out by you. That doesn't mean that you should sing as loudly as possible. It means don't pick your quietest, most subtle song for the audition.

Let's say that the audition you're going to is a typical national talent search: you'll be singing a 60 second a cappella version of your song for one person after waiting for several hours outside. Several other singers may be singing nearby. You'll be tired, hungry, and you may need a bathroom break. You know going in that the vast majority of the singers auditioning won't make it past the first round. How can you make a good impression given that these might be the worst audition conditions ever? Here's how:

Preparing for open auditions from start to finish

Research the wait

When you're researching the event try to find out what the waiting environment will be like. Knowing what's coming can make the experience easier and can even make it fun. I tell students of mine who are going to huge national auditions to expect a circus-like atmosphere. Will you need an umbrella, extra layers of clothes, sunscreen? Should you take your favorite energy bar and a water bottle? How long will you be waiting? If you'll be outside and there's any chance of cold weather be sure to bring a scarf to keep your throat and vocal cords warm, and perhaps a thermos of hot herbal tea with honey.

Prepare your performance

Every topic in this book up to here pertains to your audition. Work every vocal and physical detail of your song, if possible on camera. Practice with backing tracks, then as soon as possible just sing your 60-second version a cappella. By the way, that's usually a verse and a chorus, but you can sing whatever section you want. Sometimes there is more energy later in a song, so find the most compelling part of your song, not necessarily starting at the beginning. Keep recording yourself to make sure that when singing a cappella you stay in tune and that your rhythm stays steady.

Be completely clear on your persona, intention and goals as a performer. Dig deep into the lyric so you can completely plunge into the song, even when surrounded by hundreds of other noisy singers.

Always prepare a second song just in case, and have a third one in the back of your mind because you never know what will happen.

Don't just prepare for the first audition. Make sure you know when a second round happens (sometimes it's the same day) and prepare for it, too. For example, as of this writing round two *American Idol* singers are filmed and asked to talk about themselves. Can you gracefully talk about yourself for 40 seconds and stand out from the crowd? Prepare what you'll say as well as what you'll sing.

Mentally prepare

Auditions are stressful, no two ways around it. The value for the people auditioning you is that they get to see how well you handle singing in a stressful environment and whether you can transcend it. To do that you'll want to be mentally prepared. Get your performance mantra in place. It's fine to be competitive. If you want, your mantra can be something like "I'm going to show everyone here what a great performance is," or "I'm the singer they've been looking for." Or you might want a mantra that helps keep you relaxed: "I feel calm and prepared in the midst of this craziness," or "I'm going to give my best performance ever and the rest is up to fate."

Mentally rehearse the audition, from having your name called and approaching the production assistant to completing your song and getting a great reaction.

When you are doing performance-level rehearsals imagine that the production assistant sitting there listening to you, possibly taking notes. Imagine that there are people nearby also singing. The more you can mentally prepare for the variables of the audition, the better. Remember that you'll probably be singing just for one person, so focus appropriately.

When I'm preparing a student for one of these auditions we often start the lesson with a performance-level version of the song, no warm up, no chitchat. I want to hear how they perform when they've just walked in the door and haven't had a chance to get centered, just like the audition.

Sing for others

One of the biggest mistakes some singers make before these auditions is not singing for others beforehand. Sing your song for anyone who has a spare 60 seconds. If you're heading out to the movies with friends make them stand there for a minute while you perform. Sing your song at a karaoke club within a week of the audition.

Have two goals

One goal, of course, is to make it past the first round. Your second goal should be to give a fantastic performance to the best of your abilities. Whether or not you are what they are looking for, being able to audition well is a vital skill for a performer to have. This probably won't be your last audition, and if you can give a great performance under trying circumstances your overall confidence as a performer will soar. It doesn't mean much in the big picture of your singing career if you get past the first round or not. A former student of mine didn't get past *American Idol* Round One a few years ago, but later on her band's major label debut album was nominated for a Grammy.

The morning of the audition

Eat a good breakfast and warm up vocally if there's time. If it's an early morning call sleep a bit longer and warm up on the way there.

What to wear

Dress in comfortable, attractive clothes. It's true that some singers in whacky costumes pass to the second round, but do they ever make it past the third round? Read the *Clothing* chapter in this book and remember that you'll be standing or sitting for a long time beforehand. Think layers, so you can handle weather changes. Also, you'll be performing fairly close to the production assistant, so you don't need to trowel onstage make-up. If you and your listener are both female and you dress too sexy, you might alienate her before you sing a note. Ditto for men. Since you don't know who your listener will be, dress in a way that both genders would like. Catherine McPhee arrived last minute in jeans for the San Francisco *American Idol* auditions and claims that she performed well because she maintained a casual attitude that went with her casual clothes.

While you're waiting to sing

Do what will most keep you centered. A student of mine still corresponds with a singer she met at an *American Idol* audition. She realized that she'd have more fun and be more relaxed if she made friends with everyone nearby, so she made a point of being outgoing and friendly. If you do this, just make sure that you don't tire your voice by talking too much or too loudly.

Another student went a different route: he wore headphones, closed his eyes, listened to music, and ignored the chaos while he waited. You know yourself— do what keeps you focused while you wait. Chat with others, zone out with an Ipod, warm up, or close your eyes and silently chant your performance mantra. At some point you should mentally rehearse your performance, especially after you get any information from people exiting about what the physical conditions are like inside. Incorporate what you learn into your mental rehearsal. However, don't take anything anyone says about who is and isn't moving on to the next round as the gospel truth. Rumors that aren't necessarily true might be flying, like "They've met their female quota, they're just looking for men now." Keep telling yourself that you are what they want. Drink lots of water to stay hydrated— other people will hold your place in line if you need to run to the bathroom.

Just before the audition

Keep breathing deeply during the last few minutes before you are called. If you have brought a pitch pipe or your track on an Ipod to give yourself your starting note, put it away before you reach the front of the line or before you might be called. When you finally get to the person who will be listening to you, make eye contact with him if possible, and say hello. If it's appropriate, you could even say something like "Boy, you must be getting tired about now," or something else that acknowledges them and the situation. That can help to wake both of you up, and just might get him to pay more attention to you. Refrain from comments that are all about you, like "Wow, I'm nervous!"

The audition

It's fine to pause, breathe, and center yourself before you begin. When the adrenaline hits we tend to plunge in, but it's amazing what one or two seconds of focusing can do.

Don't worry if your listener never looks up from his clipboard while he's listening. Maintain focus anyway. Remember to look at his forehead and not his eyes. Dive deep into the lyric and rock his world.

If your song is a love song and your listener is of the right gender, sing right to them and make them fall in love with you. Don't weird them out if they are the wrong gender though! If your song is more angry or negative you might not want to sing directly to the listener since that could come across as confrontational.

If you flub a word or hit a sour note keep going. Don't stop and ask to start over again. Recover from your mistake as swiftly as you can and get back to your delivery. The listener wants to see how well you can recover.

When you finish your song, no matter what he says, thank your listener. Today's production assistant is tomorrow's producer and you never know what impact you've made with them. You may not be right for this audition, but they may remember you in the future.

After the audition

If you make it to the next round, congratulations! All your hard work paid off. Now, get ready to start the entire process again. If you don't make it to the next round, congratulate yourself for doing something that could further your goals as a singer. A teacher of mine used to say "How many times were you rejected this week by someone in the music business? If you aren't being rejected frequently, then you aren't putting yourself out there enough!"

At some point after the audition, take a minute to evaluate your performance. Take note of what went well and what didn't. This will help you prepare for your next audition. I know quite a few singers who went to two *American Idol* auditions in different cities, thinking that the first audition would just be for practice.

Other Kinds of Auditions

There are many other kinds of auditions besides national talent searches. Some of the above will still apply, but here are some additional tips for other types of auditions.

Auditions with an accompanist

Typically, when you try out for musical theater shows you'll sing your song backed by a pianist you've never met before. Making the pianist happy is your first goal. The way to do that is to bring clear, legible sheet music, and to give clear instructions. Chord charts or lead sheets with just the melody and chord symbols written above aren't acceptable for musical theater auditions. You need all of the music written out. Make sure your music is in the right key. Don't ever expect an accompanist to transpose for you on the spot. Try not to bring a twelve-page version, and clearly mark all entrances, endings, dynamics etc. on the sheet music. You can make your accompanist very happy by backing every page of your sheet music with a folder so the sheets stand up straight on the piano. Put two pages per one opened folder, then tape the folders together so your sheet music opens like an accordion. If you have edited the song, remove as many edited-out pages as possible and clearly mark the edits. Keep the introductions and musical interludes very short since your listeners aren't there to hear what the accompanist can do.

Rehearse in advance a few words that give your accompanist an overview of the song. Something like: "Start here, right after this section jump to this section, and at the end follow me." The final thing you should do is count off the song, which gives the accompanist the tempo. Make sure to practice counting off the song. You don't want to leave the tempo up to the pianist, plus you want to show the people auditioning you that you are well-prepared and in control.

Frequently accompanists will know your song already and may just start playing it at the tempo they know. You don't have to start singing if the tempo isn't to your liking. Instead, while she's playing say to her "Try that intro again a bit slower/faster, please." Take command of the situation politely but firmly. During the short introduction you should do two things at once: ensure that the tempo is correct, while you mentally prepare for the song so that you have a strong start.

For most auditioning singers, the hardest part is singing the first few notes. Many singers are afraid of coming in at the wrong time or on the wrong note. To ease these fears, rehearse the first two phrases of your song ten times as much as the rest of the song. A solid, well-rehearsed beginning is your launching pad to a great performance.

I've heard in some cities that it's appropriate to hold your sheet music while auditioning for musicals. This can give you something to do with one hand, and can make you look like you just learned the song recently, even if you've been practicing and polishing it for months. The theory is that your auditioners will cut you some slack if they think you've just learned the song. Talk to other singers and find out what the standard practice is for your area.

I will never forget an actor who once came to me right before he went to a singing audition. He was just terrible. He hadn't fully learned the song, his singing was more like yelling, he sang lots of wrong notes, and his rhythm was erratic. I later heard from his girlfriend that he got the part! When I asked her how he pulled that off she told me "He just got in their faces and completely sold the song." Remember that it's not necessarily the best singer who gets the gig, it's the one who knocks the listeners out. I've heard that for musicals it's better to overdo it than to underdo it when performing. Most directors think that it's easier to get a performer to dial back their delivery than it is to bring a performer out of his shell.

Auditions with backing tracks

If you will be auditioning with a backing track that is on a CD, make a bulletproof version. Burn a CD of just your track so a different track isn't played by accident, and so another track doesn't start playing right after yours ends. This way you won't have to tell anyone which track to play. Play your CD on several players before the audition to make sure it plays. Don't put a paper label on it, since that can make it unplayable on some older machines. Some karaoke versions have ten seconds or more of dead space before the track starts. If you can't edit that out you'll have ten seconds of nothingness to fill. Some songs also have long musical introductions. Either way, you should plan what you'll do during that time so that you aren't just awkwardly standing there waiting. Even better, edit out the introduction, or find a friend or local recording studio who can do that for you. If the latter, it should be a fairly quick, inexpensive process.

How will you begin the song? Will you walk out while the introduction is playing, or be on stage already before the music plays? If you do the second choice, you'll want to convey the mood of the song by your posture and stance before you start singing. Either way, you'll need to tell whoever is playing your CD exactly when they should hit the "play" button.

Think about how you will end the song if there isn't an obvious ending. Many songs repeat and fade at the end, and you can't vocally fade along with it. One solution is to sing an obvious ending, and then strike a final pose while the music fades. Whatever you do, make sure to rehearse the beginning and ending of your song.

Auditioning for a band

Your personality plays a big part in this situation. The band wants a great singer, but they also want someone they'll enjoy hanging out with at rehearsals and on the tour bus. This is especially true if you're trying out as a back-up singer, since your vocals aren't as prominent. Be pleasant and friendly, and if at all possible, be funny. A guitarist friend of mine is convinced that she got several gigs because she was the funniest one in the room. Don't try to be something you're not, but keep in mind that personality counts. This is a situation when you might be able to be more honest early on and say things like "Man, I'm nervous" to diffuse the tension, provided that when the music starts you sing with conviction.

Ideally, you will have researched the band beforehand, so you'll know what the dress code is and if the audition will be run informally or not. If you haven't, this will become obvious as soon as you arrive. More often than not, if the band is running the audition it will be more informal. If the record label or management is running it, they'll be on a tighter schedule. Get a sense of the atmosphere when you arrive and act accordingly.

Frequently, when auditioning for a band you'll be given some of their songs and perhaps even some tracks without vocals to practice with beforehand. Obviously, you should practice these so that you can sing them well. Also, memorize the introductions and instrumental breaks so you have your vocal entrances down.

Make sure to interact with the band when you sing. If you're auditioning to be the lead singer they'll want someone with loads of charisma who can anchor the group, but they won't want a prima donna. Sing the song with passion, but during any instrumental sections get into what is being played and make eye contact with the players.

Chapter 18:
Forming a Performance Critique Group

If you are a beginning performer and have polished your performance to a point where you know it's time to take the leap and perform for a real audience, you have several choices. You can go slowly by using the step-by-step gradual method described in the *Handling Stage Fright* chapter. You can hit some local karaoke clubs or open mic nights. Or, you can find a performance workshop to work in front of an audience in a more controlled environment. Performance workshops can be a great in-between step before you hit a real stage, but they can be difficult to find. You'd think where I live, Nashville, Tennessee, would be full of them, but a student of mine did a search recently and found nothing. One option is to create your own group: it can take a bit of effort, but it can be lots of fun and won't cost a cent. You'll also have a support system in place for when you perform out in the real world.

Guidelines for forming your own group

1. Have 2-4 people in the group. More than that and you'll be sitting around too much.
2. Have one initial meeting before committing to four meetings. Different personalities can emerge in groups. I've watched some of the nicest people I know become either destructively critical or extremely defensive in a group critique setting. Try to weed out any toxic people before the performances start.
3. Decide on a fixed amount of meetings, like four. You can decide after the fourth meeting if you want to continue the group or hit the clubs, but it's easier for people to commit to something that isn't open-ended.
4. Meet for 2-3 hours max. Two hours is better. Performance work is very focused, tiring work, so pace yourselves.

Finding participants

Asking friends to join this group is fine, though it might be harder to discontinue the group if you find at the first meeting that the group chemistry is all wrong. To recruit other members, run an ad on Craigslist or a similar online list for your area. It could read something like this:

Young female pop singer is forming a 4-week performance peer critique group. We will perform for, support, and critique each other to work through our stage jitters and polish our individual performing chops. Please contact Sherry at sherry@sherryjones.com for more information.

I added stage jitters to the above listing because many nervous performers don't realize that other performers are often as nervous as they are. They will be less frightened of joining a performance group that has other shy singers.

Some optional additions might be:

- Female/male only, please (it might feel safer at first sticking to your own gender).
- I have a video camera.
- I'm preparing for the *American Idol* auditions (or to sing at karaoke clubs, or whatever).

Or you can save that kind of information for the follow-up email.

When people respond to your listing you can reply with an email that includes possible meeting days and times. Be more specific about where you are with performing to help you gather singers at a similar level. Mention that you have been using this book and may want to use it in the group. Working out of this or another book will optimize your productivity. It also provides structure, which puts participants at ease.

When you've found some possible members, I'd recommend that you have an initial meeting at a coffee shop or other public place. This is for safety reasons. This meeting won't count as the first trial critique session, it's just a meet & greet where you can get to know each other, discuss schedules, goals, and where you are with performing. You may want to talk about performances you've seen, or talk about everyone's favorites performers. This way you can find out everyone's preferences, and can take that into account later when they give critiques. This is also a good time to go over details such as bringing backing tracks, whether to videotape or not (I vote no to this for the first session), and how formal or informal everyone would like the sessions to be. Since you instigated this group you will be expected to run it, at least at first. However, this could be as simple as saying at each meeting "Okay, who wants to go first?"

Since these are small groups, you can meet in the room you've been practicing in. Even if it's your bedroom, it will still feel like a performance once a few faces are watching you expectantly. If someone in the group has a PA, a stage with lights, or anything like that, you should use them, but any room large enough for four people will do.

General Group Guidelines

Go over these at the initial meeting.

1. Confidentiality. What goes on in the group stays in the group. Have everyone commit to confidentiality. A verbal agreement is usually sufficient. If someone's voice cracks or they start crying while performing during one of your meetings, everyone needs to know that it stays in the room. You will build more trust between the participants and will be able to do much deeper work.

2. Constructive criticism only. Leave Simon Cowell out of your group.

3. Be punctual. Don't waste anyone else's time.

4. Everyone gets equal time performing. If you spend a lot of time with someone who has an audition the next day, make sure that everyone else gets more time spent on them at the next session. Rotate who performs first at each meeting so that everyone can experience the pressure of going first.

At the first actual critique session people may be overly polite when critiquing, and that's fine. This is a time to build trust with each other and to make sure that no one is trying to hog all of the attention. Watch for toxic people who seem to enjoy criticizing a little too much. If everyone seems genuinely nice and interested in helping each singer improve you are good to go. As you continue meeting, everyone will probably share a bit more openly. Still, try to stay sensitive to each performer's needs. Some singers may be so nervous that just performing for the others is a major feat. It may bring out self-consciousness, stiffness, and voice technique problems. For these singers, the bulk of their work will be learning to perform as competently for the group as they do when alone. They will need lots of praise and support, and may not be ready for more detailed criticism.

Others may be much more comfortable with the process and will welcome more specific criticism. Use your best judgment, err on the side of being less critical, and be kind to each other.

Format for your first meeting

1. Gather everyone's backing tracks.

2. Everyone talks about their specific goals for the night. "Anne" may be working on her stage fright. "Marc" may be working on his hand movements. "Leah" may be working on her patter. "Ali" may be working on staying in tune and maintaining focus.

3. Anne sings her song while everyone else watches. No one should take notes or look elsewhere. The group should give each performer their full attention.

4. Everyone gives Anne some constructive crits.

5. Anne sings again. It's helpful to perform again immediately instead of waiting for everyone else to perform.

6. A few more crits for Anne and then Marc goes, and so on.

A variation on this would be to have a theme for each meeting, so that everyone is working on stage patter, hand and arm gestures, or whatever.

Another variation would be for the group to replicate a typical audition atmosphere so members can prepare for being put on the spot. If this method is used, don't have singers try again immediately after crits. Instead, rotate to another singer so the first singer must try fresh later on. There are no second takes at auditions.

You can tweak this format for specific needs. For singers who are auditioning for *American Idol* or similar situations, the audience could pretend to be bored, just like many of the production assistants one sings for at those auditions.

Discuss how you are feeling about the group after four sessions. If most of you still think you have some work to do, feel free to continue meeting. Keep in mind that you will get used to each other after awhile and nerves will lessen. This is good for the performers who want to move past the fear stage and fine-tune their performances, but performers who are mostly working on their stage fright will need to find a less comfortable situation. For them it may be time to hit the open mics, coffeehouses, and karaoke venues out in the world.

Chapter 19:
Mic Technique

Even if your focus right now is to prepare for an a cappella audition, at some point in the future you'll probably be singing on a mic. Good mic technique is something virtually every contemporary performer needs to develop. The mic is your friend. It will help you project during the softer parts of your song and it can amplify your sound so you don't need to strain for volume. You can even use it to fade your voice at the end of a phrase if you can't do that vocally.

If your budget prevents you from buying a mic setup to practice with before you hit the clubs, use an empty toilet paper roll or a hairbrush to rehearse at home. Then, refine your technique later at music venues that have PAs.

Mic Basics

Most mics are unidirectional. That means that if you hold it vertically to sing, like a lollypop, it won't pick up your sound as well. In general, point the head of the mic directly at your mouth while singing. It's okay to angle it slightly from above or below your mouth.

As you've probably noticed when you sing, your lower notes are softer in volume, while your higher notes are louder— this is how the voice works. You can use the mic to even out these natural volume fluctuations by holding it closer on softer notes and farther away on louder notes. Getting comfortable with "playing the mic" like this is the essence of mic technique, and it's much easier to practice if you are actually amplified so you can hear and balance the changing volume level as you sing.

You may have seen performers "eating the mic," which is singing with their lips actually touching the mic. Not only is this unsanitary, it will not produce your best amplified sound. There is something called the "proximity effect" which will give you an unpleasant boomy sound if your mouth is too close to the mic. Conversely, if you are too far from the mic the proximity effect will give you a thin vocal tone with no body. In general, you'll get the best tone quality about 2-4 inches from the mic. This range also varies from mic to mic. When singing live, use about 3 inches as your default distance, singing as close as an inch away for softer passages and as much as a foot away for louder sections. If the mic is on a stand you can position yourself with one foot more forward than the other, which makes it easier to rock backward or forward to adjust your distance from the mic.

Remember to project your voice as you normally would. Don't sing softer just because your voice is amplified.

Another good technique to learn is how to avoid popping P's. Other plosive consonants like B can also make a popping sound as the blast of air hits the mic, but P's tend to be the main culprit. You can actually modify how you pronounce your Ps so that they have less of a tendency to pop, but I think that's too much work. Instead, when you get to a word with a P in it, especially on a loud note, sing slightly above, below, or to the side of the mic so the extra burst of air isn't going directly into the mic.

 Don't look at the mic while singing, look out at your audience. When you aren't actually singing, pull the mic away from your face, or move away from it if it's on a stand. The audience wants to see your face, and the mic obstructs it. Caution: There may be times when using a hand-held mic that holding the mic down at your side or somewhere other than where it was meant to be pointed may cause feedback. Especially avoid pointing the mic at a speaker.

Playing the Mic + Focus

Stand in front of the mirror, holding an amplified mic or a prop mic like a hairbrush. Sing your song while maintaining direct forehead focus. On louder notes pull the mic away and on softer ones bring it closer to your mouth. During pauses in-between phrases pull the mic away from your face.

If you play an instrument, use a mic (or prop) in a stand and pull your head away from the mic for louder notes and in-between phrases.

Repeat this exercise, this time employing a movable focus.

The mic is a prop that you can use as one more element of your performance. Some singers hold the mic tenderly, as if they were holding their lover's face, while others grab it forcefully. Some singers treat the mic in a stand like a dance partner and move it around the stage. Check out some of your role models to see how they work the mic. Whatever style you do, learning good mic technique will add to your effectiveness and confidence as a performer.

Chapter 20:
Clothing

One of the first things the audience will notice is what you're wearing, so it pays to think about your wardrobe. Even when I wore beat-up jeans and a T-shirt on stage, I made sure it was a great fitting pair of beat-up jeans and my coolest T-shirt. Try on some performance clothes and then use this checklist to evaluate what you've chosen.

1. Do you look good?
If you look great, your confidence will soar and you'll give a better performance. I know of singers who dress up to sing at recording sessions where no one can see them, simply because they know they sing better when they look good.

2. Do you stand out?
You want everyone to be looking at you, so wear something that commands attention. That doesn't necessarily mean that you should be covered with glitter— a great fitting suit can be charismatic, too.

3. Do your clothes fit your stage persona?
Don't wear sexy clothes if you want to project a girl-next-door image, and don't wear a suit if you want to be the next Axl Rose. If you don't know if what you're wearing projects your desired stage persona, ask a friend for a second opinion. Or, use what your role models wear as a guideline (but don't copy their outfits exactly or you'll look like a wannabe).

4. Do your clothes fit your intention as a performer?
If your intention is to put your audience at ease, dress more like them. Dress provocatively if your intention is to rattle your audience. If you want to make them laugh wear funny clothes.

5. Do your clothes fit the venue?
At larger venues go bolder and wear something that looks good from a distance. At smaller gigs and auditions wear something with memorable

details that you can see close up. Don't wear stripes or busy patterns on TV.

6. Will your clothes work with stage lights?
The perfect dress might become transparent in the wrong lighting. Also, avoid colors that wash out under the lights. My mother once informed me after a performance that what I thought was a sexy pink undershirt made me look like I was topless.

7. Can you breathe?
If the waistband is too tight you won't be able to breathe deeply and you won't sing as well. Ditto for tight necklaces, ties, vests or bodices.

8. Can you move?
Tight clothes with no give will restrict your movement. Tight clothes that stretch are fine. Wearing shoes with super high heels is just asking for trouble if you'll be moving a lot.

9. Are your clothes too comfortable?
Meaning, are they too baggy? That's fine for some styles like hip-hop, but in general, the audience wants to see your body. It doesn't matter what size you are. Queen Latifah isn't thin, but onstage she wears clothes that fit her well and show her shape, and she looks fantastic.

10. Are your clothes noisy?
Beads that clatter, bracelets that rattle, dangling tinkly earrings and anything else that makes noise when you move can be picked up by the mic. Even if you aren't on mic, if it's a small enough venue, those noises will be heard by the audience.

11. Are your clothes too warm?
Assume that you'll be heating up as the adrenaline kicks in, as you sing and move, and from the heat of the stage lights. Consider wearing layers so that you can keep warm before you hit the stage, and then peel your layers off onstage.

You might want to rehearse while wearing your performance clothes to try them out. By all means wear them if you are videotaping yourself or taking a performance workshop.

Chapter 21:
Open Mics, Piano Bars, Karaoke & Sit-Ins

There are several possible next steps for singers who want to get more performing experience in front of actual people: Open mic nights, sitting in with a band, singing at piano bars, and singing at karaoke clubs. Singing at an open mic night can often also double as an audition for the club owners. These kinds of gigs are similar to auditions in that you have only one or two songs to make your mark and win over the crowd. Also, prior to singing you'll be sitting out in the audience instead of warming up backstage.

Researching in advance

Since these are regularly occurring events, you can make a study trip in advance to check out the venue, and to see how the event works. Also, you can evaluate the other singers. If the audience loves one singer, figure out why and learn from them. It might simply be that the singer has a fabulous voice, but notice the singers who go over well because of their humor, their choice of song, their moves, or their persona. And if someone bombs, figure out why so you can learn from his mistakes. Also, find out what does and doesn't work in that particular setting. Asking the pianist to play one of your original folk songs at a jazz standards piano bar is usually a bad idea, as is playing a ten-minute dirge at an open mic when twenty people are waiting to go on after you.

Feelings of jealousy are a waste of your time and energy. Stay friendly and supportive at these events, and keep any competitive feelings to yourself. You may very well become a regular here, which is a great way to keep your performance chops honed. If you do become a regular you'll probably find yourself making friends with other regulars. Not only will this make the experience more fun, but you may find an ally who can give you honest critiques of how you're doing. Also, you never know what might happen with the people you meet at open mics. I met the bassist for my last band when we were both performing at an open mic in LA.

Befriend the host, if possible. He may also be in charge of the sound, he can frequently give you a better choice of singing slots, and he is a liaison with the club. This will be important if you're hoping to do a full set there some time in the future.

You won't have a sound check at any of these places, and there may not be a sound person to make adjustments for each singer. Even if there is, don't have a discussion with them about your sound for just one song. Take what you're given sound-wise and deal with it. Take note of other singers to see if they are all moving close to the mic, which can mean that they can't hear themselves very well. If that's the case, you can mentally prepare yourself for less-than-perfect sound so it doesn't take you by surprise.

Onstage Etiquette

When it's your turn on the mic, don't tap or blow on it to make sure it's working. Instead, say something to the crowd. This is why so many performers say: "So how's everybody doing tonight?" They are testing the microphone as well as making initial contact. If you say something a bit more original than that you might make a better first impression on the audience. If the host has just introduced you, there's no point in telling the audience your name. Think of one sentence you can say to test the mic before you step up there. You can say something nice about the previous performer. (Never say anything bad.) You can say something about the song you're about to sing, who wrote it, or why you love it ("This is a song by Sheryl Crow that always reminds me of my senior prom"). You can be off-the-wall ("Does anyone here want to buy my car?"), or succinct ("Hello, everyone, I'm glad to be here").

Talking about something related to the venue can be a good idea since it acknowledges the crowd and gets everyone in the here and now ("Have you guys tried the fish tacos here? They are awesome!"). Most of these events are pretty informal so you can get playful with your "testing of the mic" sentence ("Hey, check out the cross-eyed moose head over the door!"). My point is that the one sentence with which you test the mic can be utilized to great effect, and can help you win over your audience before you've sung one note. Of course, if your persona is more like a cool James Dean you won't say much besides a simple hello.

If you talk before singing, be brief. Typically people are waiting to go on after you and it's inappropriate to launch into an extended monologue.

Choose your song for these nights as if it's an audition— you want a song that you sound great singing *and* that will grab everyone's attention. While the audience will probably be more sympathetic than the people auditioning you at cattle-call auditions, they too have probably heard many singers of mixed abilities by the time you walk on stage. Your song can be bold, funny, passionate or deeply moving, but make it a knockout.

Open Mic Nights

Typically it's first come, first served for getting on the lineup for the night, so get there before the sign-up time unless you want to go on at midnight. On your study trip you can get an idea of how early people sign up. Your first time performing there you might want to go on as early as possible so you aren't sitting around for hours getting nervous, and before the crowd gets too big and intimidating.

If you aren't accompanying yourself you'll need to rehearse and bring your own accompanist. Make sure any guitars that will be played are in tune before you're on stage— no one wants to listen to an out-of-tune guitar or wait while you tune it.

The audience at open mic nights is usually made up of other people who have come to perform. Since they are just as wound up as you are, now is a good time for humor.

If you become a regular you can use the informal atmosphere at open mics to try out new songs and develop your ad-libbing skills. That doesn't mean that you shouldn't sing your song passionately, it just means that before and after your song your demeanor can be more relaxed.

Piano Bars

There are two primary differences between piano bars and open mics. At a piano bar a pianist is right there to accompany you, and the style of music usually leans towards jazz standards, pop standards like "Just the Way You Are," and show tunes. Even if you play piano it's usually not appropriate to accompany yourself at piano bars— the pianist runs the show. The dress code and atmosphere are a bit more formal than at open mics, especially piano bars in hotel lounges. However, I've been to a few neighborhood piano bars that were much more casual. Unless you become a regular and get to know the accompanist, performing here will feel a lot like a musical theater audition since you'll be doing it on the fly, with no rehearsal. You'll need to have a quick talk with the pianist about arrangement, then count off the tempo and dive in.

As I mentioned earlier, for musical theater auditions you should have sheet music with the entire piano accompaniment written out. For piano bars bring lead sheets instead, which just have the melody of the song written out and chord symbols above the melody. Lead sheets are rarely more than two pages per song. Make sure they are in your key, and mark any arrangement notes clearly. Often at piano bars you won't even need a lead sheet, especially if you sing a popular standard like "Misty." If you want to travel light, keep in your wallet a card with several song titles and the keys you sing them in. Memorize the lyrics for those songs, then keep copies of your lead sheets in the car in case you need them.

When you're having your brief discussion with the pianist about arrangement make sure to ask if he'll be taking a solo during the song. The typical jazz standard song form is AABA, or verse 1 - verse 2 - bridge - verse 3. The singer sings the song through once, then typically the pianist starts at the top and takes a solo over the A section. If your pianist confirms that he is going to take a solo, the easiest thing to do is to say "Okay, I'll come back in at the bridge (or B section)." So you'll sing AABA, he'll improvise through AA, you re-enter and sing the bridge and the final A section.

All this can be figured out on the fly as you sing if you just watch what the pianist does and go with it. You may get to the end of the song and he may then take off into a solo. Keep track of the melody in your head and watch him, and he'll give you a nod when it's time to come back in. If you aren't sure, I think waiting to make sure a pianist is finished with their solo is more polite then jumping in to sing, in case he thinks that he's going to play through one more section.

If you haven't worked with a pianist like this before, study how other singers at piano bars communicate with the accompanist. You'll learn things like how you can tap the top of your head when you want to signal "Start back at the top!," and how you can conduct the end of the song with hand gestures. If you're a jazz singer, you'll want to get comfortable with these nonverbal ways to communicate with your accompanist or band.

Some commercially available lead sheets for jazz standards have no introduction, nor clearly marked ending. Make sure to work with a voice teacher or musician who can help you add these to your lead sheet. If you don't do this and you're at the bar and they ask what kind of intro you want, or if they know the song and are playing it from memory, you can always say "Just play a four bar intro, and follow me at the end."

Sitting in with a Band

Sometimes clubs will have a more elaborate version of a piano bar, with an entire band backing singers who typically perform one song each. The style of music can vary from country to rock to jazz to oldies, and the atmosphere is often informal. Original songs won't work here, since these bands play cover songs. What can be nerve-wracking in these situations is that you have to very quickly communicate what you'd like to several players instead of one. Luckily, often there will be a bandleader with whom you'll talk who will then convey your plan to the rest of the band. Research these places well: some are happy to go off of your lead sheets, some only play a song in the form, key and tempo in which it was originally recorded. In the latter case, if they are familiar with your song you just need to tell them the title and perhaps the original singer, e.g.: "I'm doing the Patsy Cline version of 'Crazy'" (Since Willie Nelson and Linda Ronstadt also recorded it, among many others.)

If possible, count off the band instead of having the bandleader do it. You'll feel more in command, and the players might think that you know what you're doing and follow you more closely during the song.

Sitting in with a band can be pretty stressful. Multiple players and no rehearsal can feel like a recipe for chaos. Luckily, these bands are used to having singers sit in and pretty much know how to avoid train wrecks. If you come to check out the sit-in night in advance you'll see which performers do well. It usually boils down to song choice, ease with stepping right up and taking control, and of course singing well. Your job is to enjoy the potential chaos as much as possible, and to try to deliver a great performance regardless of how well the band works with you, how overly loud the drums are, how bright the stage lights are, etc. You can even pretend that for three minutes they really are your band and interact with them. Instead of staring off into the wings during instrumental passages, watch the guitarist as he takes a solo, smile at the bass player, and move to the drummer's beat. They will have more fun and so will you, and the audience likes to see everyone on stage having fun.

Sometimes you'll sit in with a band who knows you. Someone in the band might say "We're playing at the Tavern, come on down and sit in for a song." In this case, you'll probably be able to tell them in advance what song you're singing and in what key. You might even be able to sneak in a rehearsal if they are willing. When you arrive at the show, say hello to them and see if they can give you an estimate of when they might call you up to sing. Onstage, you'll operate much like you would at any other sit-in situation. You'll do the quickie arrangement talk down, count the song off, interact, etc. Acknowledge the band publicly. Your first words into the mic could be something like "Let's hear it for this great band!"

There's no etiquette rule that says you should not outperform your host band. If you can sing better than any of them, go ahead and shine!

Karaoke

Karaoke clubs are a great place for beginning performers to work on their performance chops. Since you can find karaoke at bowling alleys and pizza parlors, it's also a good place for underage performers to get on stage. Karaoke can have drawbacks. The sound system is sometimes substandard, making it difficult to hear yourself singing. The audience is often drunk, the song selection may be limited, and the atmosphere can feel cheesy. But if you know about all of these factors going in, you can have a lot of fun and get some valuable performing experience in a low-pressure environment. I worked with a movie actress in LA who had a huge phobia about performing as a singer. To desensitize herself she started singing karaoke at a Chinese restaurant in Hollywood after they had finished serving lunch. Her only audience was the family who ran the restaurant, which was just right for my overly nervous student.

Some people take their karaoke performances seriously, which can make a lot of sense. In music industry towns like LA and Nashville you never know who might be in the audience. Singing karaoke might put you in front of record label executives. A performance is a performance and you should always try to do your best.

Ask around or go on some reconnaissance missions to karaoke clubs in your area. Find one where the sound is decent, where it's not too smoky (since smoke will irritate your voice), and where it isn't too crowded (so you won't go on at midnight). When you've found one, check out the song list so you can plan ahead. Occasionally the song list will include the key of the song, but that's rare. Assume that it's in the key the original artist sang it, then back home figure out if that's a good key for you or if some adjustments should be made. Some regulars bring their own karaoke CDs with them. Find out during your study trip if this is an option. That way, you can practice at home with the exact accompaniment you'll have at the club. Learn how long the intro is, how long any instrumental sections are, and how it ends. Rehearse what you'll do during these sections.

You might be able to chat with the DJ and find out if and how much he can change the key of a song. Usually he can shift the key up or down four half-steps from the original key, which in music terms is a major third. The DJ may think of it as how many clicks above or below the original key you want. A half-step would be one click, a whole step is two clicks, and so on. If you need to move the key higher or lower than that, find a different song. Then pick a night, grab a friend or your performance group, and go.

There can be a lot of waiting around before you go on. Try not to get drunk even if the rest of the audience is imbibing. Yes, drinking might loosen you up, but you also might give a really sloppy performance. If necessary, duck into the bathroom and try whatever nervousness relieving method or methods you've found to work best.

Once on stage you may get a chance to greet the audience, or the DJ may start the track right as you walk on. In that case, just dive in and start your performance. If you've planned your song in advance you'll have practiced the lyrics so you won't need to look at the lyric screen. Instead, deliver the song to the audience just like any other performance. If the music is still going or fading when the song ends you can strike a pose, or just wave and walk offstage.

Chapter 22:
Low-Pressure Gigs

If you have been going to karaoke, open mics, piano bars or band sit-ins for a while as a way to get your feet wet, it might be time to look for a low-pressure gig. These are low profile, regular gigs at pizza parlors, restaurants, cafes, malls and coffee shops where you might only be glorified background music. It won't be the most ego-boosting gig you'll ever have, but it's a wonderful way to perfect your performance skills before you do more important gigs.

Advantages of a low-pressure gig

I've mentioned several times about anticipating and rehearsing what it will feel like at actual performances. This is valuable, but there's nothing like a real gig with a real audience to polish your performing abilities. If you have a nightly or weekly gig you'll be able to make improvements after each show that build as the weeks go by. Plus, your stage nerves will probably wither away.

As I wrote earlier, I had a low-pressure gig at a natural food restaurant in Santa Cruz, California that helped me overcome my intense stage fright. At that gig I played guitar and sang without a mic. I've also seen low-pressure gigs where the singer sang to backing tracks through the restaurant's PA, and others where the singer brought an accompanist and her own PA.

The owners of the venues where you will find these casual shows have them because it adds to the atmosphere of their place, and because they hope it will bring in more people. You will be paid nothing or next-to-nothing at first, but you can renegotiate after a few weeks if crowds start arriving on your night.

To find a low-pressure gig, put the word out and check the local music listings for your area. Don't assume that a place that has never had live performers before might not want some now. A student of mine asked if she could do a weekly show at her local pizza parlor and they hired her on the spot. They'd been wanting to add live music, and she was the force for change.

Recording a Demo

You might need to audition for the gig, or you might need a demo CD. Don't spend a small fortune on this demo if you don't have one since it probably won't be the last one you'll do. If you'll be singing to backing tracks, take two or three of your tracks to a local recording studio, record a vocal and they will mix it down for you. If you've practiced enough in advance it shouldn't take more than a few hours. One well-rehearsed student of mine walked out of my husband's studio in an hour with a two-song demo. That's unusually fast, so plan on more time than that. Home studios are fine for this project. Very good quality equipment is much less expensive than it used to be, so many home studios are well equipped.

If you accompany yourself or have an accompanist, take her to the studio to do a quick demo. This might take a bit longer than singing to a backing track since she'll need to record her part as well. Even so, it shouldn't take more than a few hours for two or three songs, which is all you need for this kind of demo. You can record your demo at home if you have good equipment and are proficient on it. But don't just set up a cassette recorder and sing into it— your demo needs to sound professional.

If you don't have an accompanist, you can hire one just for the demo and find another one later when you've found a gig. Many studio engineers are also accompanists, or at least know of good ones. Accompanists are also easy to find when you actually have the gig, though you will probably need to pay them, whether or not the venue pays you.

Once you've found a gig, if it's amplified, the first thing to figure out is the sound system situation. If they don't have a PA it's up to you to rent, borrow, or buy one. At smaller places this doesn't have to be a huge PA or a huge investment. There are many small PAs available these days, and the people at Guitar Center or Sweetwater would love to tell you about them. If you don't want to hassle with PAs, limit your gig search to places that are small enough not to need them, or places that already have one.

Onstage etiquette

Okay, you've found the gig, you've worked up a set or two of songs, and you're at the show. The main thing to figure out is if you are background music, or if people are actually watching and applauding you after each song. If it's the former, keep any stage patter to a minimum and consider yourself a human jukebox. People may be listening, but don't treat this as an official show that's all about you. The venue owners want your singing to add to the ambiance. You can still do your act as if the audience were watching carefully and think of it as a live rehearsal. Or you can tone down your delivery a notch since you aren't being intently watched. Whether or not you have audience, you should look like you're having fun singing.

If the audience *is* listening to you, go ahead and talk in-between songs, if you like. Use this as a place to not only work on your stage moves, but also your stage patter. I'll address this topic more deeply in the *Stage Patter* chapter.

Depending on the atmosphere of the venue, you may need to change the energy level of your set. If you're at a noisy bowling alley you may want to amp up the energy, and if you're at a quiet cafe you'll want to tone things down. Choose your songs accordingly. You can still keep the stage persona you settled on earlier, but it may be a more casual version of your persona, like Bon Jovi when he does sit-down acoustic sets.

Even though this may be a more casual venue, give as good a performance as you can. You never know to whom you'll be singing. While singing to tracks at a Mexican restaurant, a student of mine was discovered by a big songwriter. A producer heard an LA friend at a Hamburger Hamlet. He liked one of her songs and had the artist he was producing cut it. It was big hit and she bought a house with the proceeds!

Back-up gigs

Another way to get onstage experience in a less pressured way is to be a back-up singer. For this, you'll need good harmonizing skills and a team player attitude. You won't be able to practice your lead singer moves or stage patter since your job will be to support the lead singer, but you'll acquire invaluable experience. Before her career took off Shawn Colvin toured as Suzanne Vega's back-up singer. In later interviews she said she'd learned all about being a professional performer on *and* off stage by observing Vega.

Chapter 23:
Sound Checks & Sound During the Show

Sound check etiquette

Sound checks, when the mics and everything else that is amplified are tested, can take several forms. They can be fairly relaxed affairs that happen in the late afternoon, before dinner and the actual show. They can be more rushed, done right before or as the audience files in. And sometimes they are done on the fly immediately before you sing. How a sound check goes can set the mood for a performance, so you want to do what you can to help it run smoothly. You can also use your sound check to develop good communication with the sound person.

Making your sound person happy is always in your best interest. Always be polite and friendly with them, and never consider them your servant. I often tip my sound person before the show to show my appreciation. I brought a bag of cookies for the sound person the first time I performed at the Bluebird Cafe in Nashville and we've been pals ever since.

Level, reverb & EQ

Most PA's have two kinds of speakers: the mains, which face away from the stage and send the sound out to the audience, and the monitors, which face the performers and send the sound towards them. Your first concern is the monitor, since you want to be able to hear yourself. When it's time to test your mic, don't tap or make a "ch" sound into it, just speak into it to make sure it's on. Then sing a phrase at performance level volume to get a true sense of the level. Of course, if you sing loudly put some distance between you and the mic. If you are playing with musicians who gradually increase their volume during the course of the show, either by turning up their volume knobs or just playing harder, stay a couple of inches further from the mic than you'll be in performance. That way, if you're being drowned out you'll be able to boost your own level by getting closer to the mic. If you do this during the show you risk being too loud for the mic and distorting, but I think it's worth the risk.

The three things you're listening to on the monitor are volume level, reverb and tone quality, or EQ. (Often sound checks are run quickly and the most you'll do is get a good volume level, but I'll discuss all three elements in case you have more time.) If you can't hear yourself, it's helpful to be specific with your requests and say something like "Please turn me up in the monitor 25% more." If you're playing an instrument you'll need to specify for both, for example "Could I get 10% more guitar and 10% less vocal, please?"

Reverb is an echo effect that can be added to your voice to simulate a larger space, like a concert hall. Some singers like lots of it, while some want as little as possible. I prefer less reverb or a "drier" vocal since I think it helps me stay more in tune. You can request more or less reverb in your monitor mix just as you make volume level requests. Sometimes the sound person can give each performer in a group a separate monitor and separate mix, and sometimes everyone gets the same mix. If the latter is the case, it's critical that you can hear yourself in the mix. Don't compromise. It's also important that you can hear whatever instrument you tune to. That's usually the keyboard or guitar, not the bass and obviously not the drums. You need to hear enough drums to keep your tempo solid and no more. As most singers in bands will tell you, hearing enough drums in the mix is usually not the problem, it's hearing too much of them.

If you are singing to a track, you can't make requests like "I need 20% less bass in the monitor, please." All you can request is more or less of your vocal and/or the track.

The "EQ" is the tonal mix you hear. If the higher frequencies are turned up your voice will sound brighter and "treble-y" and will cut through the other instruments. If the lower frequencies are turned up your voice will sound beefier and warmer. A good EQ mix balances these elements. If you have the time and the know-how during a sound check you can request EQ changes as you would volume and reverb changes. Even though this is not the mix the audience will hear, (the sound person will decide that), there are two reasons to spend time doing this. Firstly, the better the EQ, the easier it is to hear your voice in relation to the instruments and thereby stay in tune. Secondly, a good EQ mix brings out the good qualities of your vocal sound. When your voice sounds good to you through the monitors your confidence goes up. I'm convinced that some of my best performances were largely because my voice and guitar sounded so good in the monitor mix, and I know that lousy monitor mixes played a big part in my less successful performances.

During more leisurely sound checks I usually have someone I trust stand in the room to see what the sound is like coming out of the main speakers. They check that mix to make sure that my vocals aren't drowned out by the instruments, and that the reverb and EQ levels seem right. The sound will change somewhat when the audience fills the room, but this still gives me a chance to convey any requests to the sound person.

If there are multiple performers playing that night, remember that they each will have their own mixes. I've headlined shows where the sound check went smoothly, but by the time the opening act played and I got onstage the sound person had forgotten my settings and the mix for me was completely different. Sometimes when I'm co-headlining a night I'll request that I open the show to avoid this problem. Of course, as bands and artists become more successful they often bring their own sound person with them to every gig, which provides much greater control of the sound.

Using the sound check to prepare psychologically

The sound check gives you a chance to get your bearings onstage before the show. Notice potential distractions you may need to deal with during the show. Some things, like a TV by the bar, you can request to have turned off during your show. Other things, like a noisy bar close to the stage, can't be changed, but at least can be anticipated so the noise level doesn't take you by surprise later on. Notice any unusual artwork or decor you can comment on during your show. Get a feel for the stage and how much room you have to move. Notice the size of the room and if it has a balcony or seats far on the side you'll want to include. Most importantly, imagine, even if only for a few seconds, what it will feel like to sing when the audience has filled the seats. This mental preparation can help ease any nervousness you may have, and can ease the initial shock some performers have when they first walk onstage and face the audience.

Sometimes you simply don't have time to make lots of requests at a sound check. I've done shows where I set up right after the previous performance, tested the mics for 10-60 seconds, and then launched into my set. When you're in that situation it's not appropriate to make loads of sound requests. Get rough volume levels, squeeze in a reverb level request if you can, forget about EQ requests, and go.

During normal sound checks, check two (or fragments of two) varied songs if possible, for example a soft ballad and a loud high-energy wailer. When the sound check occurs during a show with the audience right there, I prefer checking with something I won't be performing that night. I don't want to give anything away, so when the sound person asks me to sing, I sing two phrases of a song that isn't in my set.

Sometimes an artist will maintain two different personas at during-the-show sound checks, one for the sound check and one for the performance. Even at more casual shows at smaller venues, some performers refuse to diffuse the power of their performance by taking part in the on-the-fly sound check. They have someone else check the mic for them so they can make their entrance when their set actually begins. I try to do what's appropriate for the level of the show. If it's a more casual show I act polite and businesslike during the quickie sound check, always staying aware that some people in the audience are already watching me. Then I let my stage persona take over for the actual show. At more prestigious shows the sound check often happens long before the audience arrives so this isn't always an issue, but it's worth thinking about in advance so you aren't taken by surprise. Checking out the venue and their sound check policy in advance is always a good idea.

During Your Performance

The sound person is often making lots of little adjustments when you first hit the stage, and sometimes you'll notice sound issues during the first one or two songs of your set. If I'm doing a whole set I'll try to make any quick sound requests after the first song, and I try to address the sound person by name. I personally never make EQ requests during a show, just volume and reverb requests. Once onstage, I take whatever EQ I'm given.

When I lived in LA, my band regularly played a neighborhood club where the sound person mixed the vocals too low despite our repeated requests. So after the first song I'd ask the audience if they could hear my vocals. If enough people called out "No!" the sound guy turned me up. This probably didn't make me popular with the sound guy, but it got me the vocal level I wanted.

If you're in a band, remember that anyone playing an electric instrument has a volume knob they can and probably will use during the set to make their own sound adjustments. Also, any player can strum or hit their instrument harder for more volume. The sound person can't control this, so it's critical that you have performance level rehearsals with your band to iron out these problems in advance. This is one area where you need to stand firm as a singer. The audience wants to hear your vocals, and the band is your accompaniment. Not all players realize this; a bass player told me years ago that he was positive that everyone came to our shows to hear him and not me, though I was the singer and songwriter. If any player starts to drown you out during the performance you may strain your voice to be heard and the show will suffer. Communication with your band members about appropriate sound levels is vital, and it needs to happen long before you hit the stage. I know artists who have fired their guitarists and drummers because these players simply couldn't do anything but play at full volume during a show.

Signaling the sound person

Let's say you're singing your first song and you realize that your voice is too soft and the guitar (yours or another player's) is too loud in your monitor. If you're only singing one or two songs you'll need to communicate your requests quickly. Keep singing, and during a pause in the vocal look towards the sound person. Point at your mouth, then point up to request more vocal volume. Point down if you want less. Then point at the guitar and point down. Remember that if the guitar is running through a separate amp your sound person can't change the level, and you'll need to make the same gesture towards the guitar player and hope that he will turn down.

If you want more or less overall volume in the monitor, point at it and point up or down to make volume requests. If you are wearing an ear monitor, point at it and then point up or down. Don't interrupt your performance with loads of these gestures, but use them if you really need some sound changes. If the sound person ignores your request you can gesture a second time, but after that just live with the sound and do the best you can. If you've ever watched the Grammies you've seen that even the biggest stars have to cope with monitor problems, but at shows this big you won't see them gesturing towards the sound person.

I know many rock singers who can never hear themselves well during shows because the instruments are so loud. Many of these singers wear an earplug in one ear so they can hear themselves better. I used to do this with my rock band, and I've also worn an earplug for back-up gigs where I knew my vocal would be mixed very low in the overall monitor mix.

Sometimes you'll see an artist cupping one of her ears during a performance. This also signals the sound person that she can't hear herself well. I've sung back-up gigs where I cupped my ear for most of the show. I knew that my monitor mix was low on the sound person's priority list, and I preferred to stay in tune by cupping my ear. If I'm singing lead I rarely cup my ear since presumably I'm the focal point and it's a visual distraction.

Take note of the sound quality during the show, and get some feedback from people in the audience afterward. If this is a hometown gig you'll want to keep track of which venues have the best sound and sound people. Some venues simply have terrible sound no matter how well you communicate with the sound person, and you'll need to decide if putting up with mediocre sound is worth playing at that venue again. While it's a valuable skill to be able to perform well in spite of crummy sound, if there's a choice you may want to find a venue with better sound for your next show.

Chapter 24:
Stage Patter

You rehearse and rehearse your songs until your set seems to be a polished gem, but have you rehearsed what you will say to the audience? If you're in a musical theater show or a carefully worked-out choreographed production everything you say may be scripted, but most performers at some point find themselves talking unscripted to an audience. I realized long ago that it wasn't my singing that made me nervous at a show, it was my lack of stage patter skills. Once I worked on them my entire performance rose to a new level.

How much to talk

How much or how little you say to the audience will be dictated by your style of music, your performing intentions, and your persona. If you're a folksy singer-songwriter you may talk a great deal to the audience during the course of your set. If you're doing bar gigs with a band you probably won't be doing long monologues. If you're a singer playing larger auditoriums you may talk less, since a bigger audience calls for a bigger production, or you might talk more to add some intimacy to the show. Elton John did the latter when I saw him at an arena show last year. Even if you're in a loud rock band that does a highly music-driven show with very little speaking, you still need to be comfortable with a bit of talking. What if your guitarist breaks a string? You'll need something to fill the time, and that's where patter comes in.

Think about your persona and intentions as a performer and get an idea of how much talking belongs in your set, whether a great deal or just a few words.

Patter can work two ways. One way is to enhance the mood you're trying to create. For example, if you're in a high-energy dance band you may shout out a line like "Let's get moving now!" A punk band might say something confrontational to get the audience riled up. A funny songwriter might tell funny stories. A sexy songstress might say things she'd say to a lover, like "I'm feeling a little wild tonight!"

Patter can also be used to soften or add depth to your persona. A cabaret singer who only sings heart-wrenching slow ballads might make some witty comments in-between songs so the audience sees another side to her. Get an idea of what you want your stage patter to do for you and your audience.

Patter Research

Watch four concert sets by your role models. Make sure that your role model talks a bit in-between songs, even if it's just a few words. You can fast-forward through the actual songs and just listen to the patter if you like. You can do this research at live shows, too. Answer the following questions about each set you watch.

1. Did the performer talk a little or a lot?

2. Did the patter help to increase the mood created by the songs, or did it create a different one?

3. Did the performer have the same or different personas when singing vs. talking?

a. If different, was this effective?
4. In general, was the performer's patter: serious, funny, theatrical, flirtatious, down-to-earth, or something else?

5. Did the performer's patter sound like what a lot of other performers say or did it have a unique style?

6. Is this the kind of patter you could see yourself using?

Answering these questions will give you a better idea of what kind of patter is right for your set.

Good stage patter can help your performance stand out from the pack. Many performers who haven't thought about their stage patter in advance end up saying the same old tired phrases. How many times have you heard a performer say "How's everyone doing tonight?" While the intention to engage the audience is good, surely there's a more original way of asking the same question. Songwriters who talk about the writing of each song tend to say "I wrote this song when..." Go ahead and talk about what inspired the song, but find another way to introduce it.

Some clichés can be useful. If you're on tour, "Hello Kansas City!," (or whatever town you're in), is a great way to acknowledge the crowd and show that you actually know where you are.

At larger shows performers sometimes say less and speak more slowly since the sound can be boomier and the crowd noise might cover more elaborate sentences. Sometimes brevity works better.

Eight things to talk about with the audience

1. Physical aspects of the venue. Is there art on the walls? Are you outdoors under a blanket of stars? Mentioning something about the environment helps the audience focus on the here and now and personalizes your comments so they don't think you say the same thing at every show.

2. Talk about the song you're about to sing. Don't give the audience a blow-by-blow of the entire song since you're about to sing it. Instead, tell them something that could add to their appreciation of it. Tell them something about the songwriter, or some historical information if it's an older song. Or talk about why the song moved you so much when you first heard it. If you wrote the song you can talk about what inspired you to write it.

3. Talk about something that relates to the theme of the song. At a show last year I told the audience about my father finding love and getting married at age eighty, then I sang a hopeful love song. The song wasn't inspired by my dad, but his story was still a good lead-in.

4. Talk about yourself. It can be very effective to reveal some personal information about yourself to the audience, who hopefully will feel closer to you for it. At a performance competition, I once watched a gorgeous singer-songwriter with messy blond hair win over the crowd by opening her set with "Man, this is one bad hair day."

5. Talking about yourself can backfire if it becomes clear that it's all you ever do. Make sure to balance personal comments with ones that are more inclusive of the audience.

6. Talk about the weather. It's the universal icebreaker.

7. Talk about current events. I scan the newspaper headlines the day of a gig to see if there's something I can talk about that night.

8. Talk about your band. When Chris Isaak was still playing smaller clubs, he'd launch into long funny stories about weird deeds done or strange clothes worn by someone in his band. Since his set included a lot of slow, sad love songs, this also gave his audience a break from too much heartache.

9. Talk about the crowd. "I'm seeing some great dancers out there tonight!"

At some point during your set you should acknowledge both your band and the crowd. Make sure everyone in the band at some point is introduced and applauded, and thank the audience for coming out to the show. At smaller shows I often thank the sound person as well, and at dinner shows I encourage everyone to tip their waitperson generously.

Years ago, when I was less comfortable with stage patter, I would look at my set list in advance and figure out every single thing I wanted to say in-between songs. I'd jot a few reminder words in-between the song titles for when I was onstage. Then when I practiced entire sets by myself I'd practice talking as well. Other artists practice during daily life. A singer-songwriter pal of mine was telling me a long funny story last year when I realized that she was trying out the story on me before telling it to an audience!

It can also help to think of a few things to say during unplanned pauses in the show, like if the guitarist needs to tune, or if you need to take off your jacket. The more prepared you are for "covering" when unforeseen problems occur onstage, the less they will throw you off-balance.

If you're rehearsing with other people it can feel silly to practice what you'll say to the audience. Instead, if there's a pause in-between songs just think about what you might say during a real performance.

What *not* to say

The list of what *not* to say is endless, but it boils down to this: don't insult your audience, and don't waste their time. Use your common sense. Your audience has chosen to spend some of their time with you, which is a great gift. In return, you should try your best to make that time worthwhile. They want to be entertained, inspired, amused, or moved. You can do that both with your songs and with your patter.
Unless they're all masochists, they *don't* want to be bored, irritated, or insulted. Recently I watched two hapless performers at a small club here in Nashville. The first was having a nightmare performance— she broke a guitar string, and then couldn't keep the new string in tune. I've seen this happen dozens of times to singer-songwriters and have seen what to do: tell a funny story (memorized for just such occasions) while re-tuning the guitar. Instead, this performer got frustrated, stopped halfway through her song, said "This just isn't working" to the audience, and walked offstage, never to return. I will definitely remember her, but not in a positive way. The second performer kept swearing and insulting the audience and the sound person. It was a toss-up which performer came off worse!

Some artists are extremely uncomfortable with stage patter despite fame and experience. A student of mine saw Barbra Streisand perform live and told me that everything she said to the audience was read off of a teleprompter. My student thought this made the entire performance feel artificial, but Streisand is known to have world-class stage fright and clearly she was taking no chances. I've seen other performers who are so at ease onstage that they walk on unprepared and just start riffing off the top of their heads. Most performers fall somewhere in-between these two extremes, and find that a little patter planning and rehearsal can make the entire performance go much more smoothly.

Interviews

What if you're preparing for an audition or variety show appearance and they ask you about yourself after you sing? It pays to prepare what you might say. The people auditioning you or the variety show audience want to see how poised you can be both singing *and* speaking.

Interview Rehearsal

You can either recruit a friend to play your interviewer or simply imagine that someone is asking you the following question during an audition or while being interviewed on a variety show.

"Tell us something about yourself."

Mentioning where you're from often works, but try to think of some things about you that are a little different and will make you memorable. "I'm from Little Rock, I just spent three years in the Peace Corp and ever since I've been back I've been eating Rocky Road ice cream every single day." You can be more immediate: "I played Bruce Springsteen CDs and jumped rope for an hour before I came here." Tell us things you *do* instead of what you *are*. It can sound really goofy to say "Everyone says I'm a dreamer!" If you say "I like to go to the airport and watch the planes take off, and wonder where they're going," you'll get a similar feeling across in a more descriptive way.

You can stretch this exercise further by answering questions like: "What's been going on with you lately?" and "Tell us something that got you really excited recently." The point is to rehearse some responses to typical questions so that at actual interviews you don't say "well, um, I grew up in Boise, and, um, I really like to sing, and...."

If you're doing this exercise with a friend, direct your answers to them and maintain eye-to-forehead contact as you would when focusing on someone in the audience. If you're working alone, work with a mirror and speak to yourself to make sure your facial and body movements are poised and confident while you're speaking.

Chapter 25:
Pacing Your Set

If you're doing more than one song in a row at your performance you are doing a set. Each song you do can influence how the next one is received. Whether you're doing a set of three or thirteen songs, there are some commonly agreed upon rules of what usually works when building and pacing a set. You can go against these guidelines if you like, but for a greater chance of success when performing you should at least know the rules so you can break them intelligently.

Pacing tips

Your first song should be uptempo, easy to sing, and easy to hear. The audience is checking you out visually, deciding if they like what they see, and deciding if you know what you're doing. They are not yet carefully listening to you, so this is not the place for a wordy or complex song. I love starting with a song I can sing fairly loudly since it gives me somewhere to channel all the adrenaline that has built up before the show. If you're like most performers, if you get a case of nerves it will be strongest for the first number. Don't add to your nervousness by starting with a difficult song, especially since the audience isn't ready to hear one yet.

Frequently, singers say hello to the audience after the first or second song. Some bands will play through several songs without a break before saying a word. See what your role models do, and also let your intentions guide you as to where and where not to speak.

By the second song, the audience is hearing what you do a bit more, but still isn't listening super carefully to you. Stay medium to uptempo if possible, and if you are doing a 30-40 minute set, hold off on the slower or more challenging songs. By your third song, the audience is ready to settle in and really listen, so you can do your first slower song or ballad.

Your 'heavier' songs can live in the middle of the set. Then build towards your closing song. This song should be a whopper that leaves your audience wanting more.

If you get an encore you know the audience is very receptive to hearing more from you. Performers use an encore in different ways. Some do a quiet, meaningful song since the audience is enthusiastic and listening carefully. Others continue the up mood by doing another high-energy song. Others sing a left-of-center or playful song that doesn't fit well into their normal set. You have lots of room to move if you get an encore, but this is not a good time for lengthy stage patter. The audience wants to hear one or two more songs from you, not a monologue.

For three-song sets you can compress this set plan. Open with an easy uptempo, sing a ballad, and end with a splashy leave-them-wanting-more song.

More pointers for pacing your set

- Don't put two ballads back-to-back. Revive your audience after each slow song with a mid- or uptempo song. Unless you do trance music, vary the tempo from song to song throughout the set.

- Don't put two songs in the same key back-to-back. I know artists who make sure each song is followed by a song in a slightly higher key, for example: Song 1 key of G, then song 2 in the key of A, followed by song 3 in the key of Bb, and so on. Most of the audience won't notice these key changes, but they will unconsciously feel how the entire set keeps rising.

- Don't put two songs with the same theme back to back. If you follow a sad love song with two more sad love songs your audience may want to slit their wrists. If your entire set is made up of sad love songs, break up the mood with some lighter patter.

- My friend Kristina Olsen, a wonderful performer, reminded me that the audience is often sitting still and breathing shallowly during a show. After about thirty minutes or so they need reviving with more oxygen. This is why so many performers have a sing-along around then since it gets everyone breathing deeply again. Another option is to tell a funny story and get them laughing, or do a dance song that gets them clapping or moving.

- Remember to accept any applause you receive by nodding, thanking the audience, bowing, or with some other gesture. This is especially important at the end of your set. The audience is acknowledging you with their applause and it's rude to ignore that acknowledgment.

Pacing and your voice

It also pays to take your voice into consideration as you build your set. Save the songs with the highest or most difficult notes for later in the set so you can warm up for them with the earlier, easier songs. If you have a fast or wordy song that leaves you a bit out of breath, follow it with a song that has lots of breathing space so you can recover. Follow a busy dance routine with a ballad for the same reason. Singing your set is like running a marathon; you don't want to run top speed right out of the gate, you want to pace yourself so your vocal strength lasts for the entire show. I mentioned earlier that your vocal range may shift slightly higher in performance due to increased adrenaline. Depending on your voice and your vocal technique, it may also shift up during the course of a set. Therefore, songs with notes that are very low in your range belong earlier in the set. Low notes require a kind of vocal control which is easier for most singers to attain *after* the first one or two adrenaline-charged songs, so put those low songs early in your set, but not first.

As for the length of the your set, I think shorter is better than longer. Yes, Bruce Springsteen can play all night and the audience will love him, but he's one of the exceptions. Most people have short attention spans. It's better to do a tight, fantastic forty-minute set than an hour-long set with a lot of filler.

Chapter 26:
Repertoire

Repertoire Building

Your repertoire is all of the songs you know, and all the songs in each set you perform come from your repertoire. Earlier we discussed song selection and the importance of knowing your persona, intention, and goals as well as your vocal strengths and limitations when you selected or wrote a song. These remain important as you build your repertoire. You can see from the previous chapter that if you are putting together a set of songs you have some additional concerns. These include having a variety of tempos, keys, and moods in your set. If you are in the process of building your repertoire, it's helpful to analyze what kinds of songs you do and don't yet have so that you can create a good balance of material.

Every song conveys a mood, story, and personality. The sum of all the songs in your set conveys a broader statement about you. The beauty of singing a set of songs is that each song is just one element in the bigger picture of you, the artist. For example, if you had never heard of Stevie Wonder and all you heard him perform was "I Just Called To Say I Love You," you might think that he was a performer of heartfelt, easy-listening songs. But what if he did a set that included that song *and* "Higher Ground," "Living for the City," "All In Love Is Fair," and "Signed, Sealed, Delivered"? You'd realize that he can break your heart, get spiritual, have fun, *and* give biting social commentary. Now that's a deep artist.

Whether you are currently building your repertoire or you already have a full set of songs that you're performing, use these next two exercise to take a look at what you've got.

Initial Repertoire Analysis

Write down every song in your current repertoire. If you have an extensive repertoire, just pick your twenty favorite songs. Scan the titles, and then answer these questions. Among your songs, do you have:

1. A good opening number?

2. A good second song? (Reread the last chapter if you need more information on what will and won't work.)

3. A meaty mid-set song?

4. A strong closer?

5. A wonderful encore?

The Statement Your Set Makes

You've already analyzed each song to make sure that it fits your persona, intention and goals. Now look at the sum of all these songs and analyze how they work as a set:

1. Does this group of songs add up to a statement about you as an artist?

2. What is that statement?

3. Is that what you want to tell the world?

> 4. If not, would adding or subtracting a song or songs from the group give a better statement?
>
> 5. What kind of song(s) do you still need in your repertoire: Uptempo? Heartbreaking? Vocally impressive? Funny? Deep?

You may have realized that you didn't have a strong opener or a killer heart-wrenching ballad. Or, you may have seen that you're on the right track as you add new songs. Later, you'll take your analysis a step further.

The Audience Response

Obviously, two ways your audience experiences you is to see you and hear you. But it's helpful as you analyze your repertoire to be aware of the other ways your audience experiences you.

- Body: feeling rhythm in one's body is a primal, non-thinking experience.

- Intellect: your brain processes language. Your song lyrics and stage patter can tickle and delight the brain if they are intellectually satisfying.

- Heart: People want to be moved emotionally. The music and lyrics of your songs, and your delivery of them, can have an emotional punch that touches people deeply.

A truly satisfying song or performance often has all three of these elements in play. For example, at first listening some rap songs appear to be all about rhythm and nothing else. But Eminem and many other rappers use intellectually satisfying intricate wordplay as they perform songs that tell emotionally moving stories. A classic Hank Williams song may at first listening seem to be all sappy emotion. But the steady rhythm of his songs can hook the body's rhythm response, and the elegantly well-crafted lyrics satisfy the mind.

As you evaluate your repertoire see if there's a balance of these three elements.

The Evolving Repertoire

Performing artists frequently examine, add to, and subtract from their repertoires. There are several reasons they do this:

- **Change of persona.** After Prince became a Jehovah's Witness he removed several of his earlier, racier songs from his performing repertoire. He realized that some of his older songs didn't jibe with his new, less sexually overt stage persona. An artist with a long career may alter his persona subtly or greatly over time. Since the songs he sings convey that persona, his repertoire would need to change as well. Queen Latifah's repertoire now includes rap, R&B and jazz standards, reflecting how as her persona has evolved over the years.

- **Change of intention.** Bruce Springsteen has changed his intention on several of his tours. Sometimes his intention (or one of them, at least) is to rev up his fans, so he plays energetic, passionate songs. On other tours his intention is to have his audience think, so he plays quieter, more reflective songs.

- **Change of goals.** A rock singer who decides she wants to wear a fancy dress and sing at jazz clubs would need to learn a set of jazz standards. A poet-folksinger who realizes he wants to make more money and play to bigger crowds might start writing and performing more commercial pop songs.

- **Balance & Pacing Improvements.** As artists become more aware of the power of a well-paced set, they find the necessary ballad, uptempo song, or whatever else that better fleshes out their set.
- **Audience Response & Desires.** Sometimes that song you just loved singing at rehearsal falls flat with the audience. Or perhaps

one time only you sing a Dylan song at a Dylan tribute show and the audience goes insane, so you add that song to your set. As artists perform more, they discover which songs go over better with their audience and take that into consideration. Ray Charles virtually always sang "Georgia" at his concerts because he knew his audience would leave disappointed if he hadn't sung it.

- **Repeat Customers.** Though you may have hits you'll always want to keep in your set, your audience doesn't want to hear *all* the same songs over and over again. If you stick to the same set for too long, you risk losing fans who want to hear something new from you.

- **Staying Inspired & Fresh.** Artists get sick of their set, too. You may come up with the perfectly balanced and paced set, but after several months of touring it becomes hard to sing some of the songs with fire and authenticity. If you can't wake up your passion for those songs by reanalyzing the lyric or changing the arrangement, it may be time to retire them for awhile.

- **Vocal Difficulties.** Some songs don't become problematic until they are sung live. During a long demanding tour, or if you are singing while sick, the lowest or highest notes in some songs may be too difficult to reach. Easier songs should then join your set.

If you have a repertoire of ten or more songs that you can perform, do the following exercise to analyze whether they create a good set.

More Repertoire Analysis

List ten to fifteen songs from your current repertoire. After each one, note the key (if you know it), the tempo (slow, medium or uptempo), and the feel (swing, ballad, waltz, reggae, etc.). Also list the mood (happy, sad, pensive, angry, etc.), vocal difficulty, and where it might belong in your set (opener, encore, etc.)

Song Title	Key	Tempo	Feel	Mood	Vocal Ease	Placement
1.						
2.						
3.						
4.						
5.						
6.						
7.						
8.						
9.						
10						
11						
12						
13						
14						
15						

When you look at your song list this way you may realize that you have way too many ballads, or songs in the key of C, or easy songs. That doesn't necessarily mean you have to dump any of them, but they may not all belong in the same set. Though sometimes you can intersperse similar songs throughout your set, you may find that you need to rotate similar songs in different sets. For one of his recent tours, Van Morrison's band learned well over one hundred of his songs. Then he changed the set for each show.

If you're seeing too many similar songs on your list, note which ones are the strongest and move on to the next exercise.

Set Building

Take the songs from the list you just made and reorder them to create a set. Put your best opening song at #1, put your closer and encore songs at the end and fill in your set from there. If you eliminated some songs from your last list because you had too many repetitions, you have several choices. You can shorten the entire set, or leave some of the slots blank and note what is needed for each position in the set (e.g. uptempo easy song for the opening slot). If you have other songs in your current repertoire, see if you can find one that will work here. Like the others, analyze it for key, mood, tempo, etc., to make sure it will work.

	Song Title	Key	Tempo	Feel	Mood	Vocal Ease	Placement
1.							
2.							
3.							
4.							
5.							
6.							
7.							
8.							
9.							
10.							
11							
12.							
13.							
14.							
15.							

Don't make yourself crazy striving for variety. For example, you can probably have a couple of songs in the same key back-to-back if they vary enough in tempo or feel. Which kinds of songs can be repeated more will also vary, depending on the kind of performer you are. A torch singer can get away with lots of sad love songs. A diva in top form can do a run of vocally demanding songs. Use the above exercise as a guide for avoiding too much repetition in your set, but also use your best artistic judgment and knowledge of what your strong suit is as you make your choices.

After analyzing your repertoire and completing the above exercises, you hopefully have created a well-paced, powerful set. At the very least, you'll know what kinds of songs are needed to fill any gaps in your repertoire.

Chapter 27:
Performance Preparation: Everything Else

Giving a great performance involves a slew of preparatory elements besides rehearsal and mental preparation. Here are some of the factors that can affect your voice and performance, along with some helpful tips.

Sleep & diet

Sleep: Plan ahead so that you get ample sleep, 7-8 hours of it, the night before a show. Many singers sing flat when they are sleep-deprived. Naps can help if your sleep habits are irregular, but remember that your vocal cords will also take a nap and relax. Wait to warm up until *after* a nap so you don't have to warm up twice.

Diet: Experiment with different foods to find out what gives you energy, but doesn't make you feel so full that you can't breathe easily. Though I rarely eat them on non-show days, I like eggs for my pre-show meal since they provide energy but aren't too filling.

Try a bigger meal earlier in the day and a smaller one two hours before the show. Singing takes a lot of energy, so don't starve yourself. Eat as if you were an athlete before a game or track meet.

Avoid dairy products before you sing, which can cause mucous. Also avoid throat irritants like coffee, overly spicy foods, and alcohol. If you have food allergies, definitely avoid those foods the day of your show since they can also cause mucous and fatigue. Some common food allergies are lactose, wheat, and corn. Many people don't have true food allergies, but instead have mild sensitivities to certain foods like bananas or red peppers. These foods can make you burp or give you gas, neither of which you'll want to happen onstage. Avoid any foods to which you are sensitive for six hours before a show.

Hydrating your vocal cords

Drink as much water as possible throughout the day, at least eight glasses at room temperature— cold water will constrict the vocal cords. Your vocal cords like to be kept warm and moist. Herb teas with honey can be helpful since they provide steam, plus the honey soothes the throat. But you should experiment to find out which herb teas work for you. Just because a tea is herbal doesn't necessarily make it good for you. Singers with ragweed allergies can react negatively to peppermint tea, for example.

Anything carbonated will fill you up too much, make you burp, and make it harder to breathe deeply. Many people think lemon and honey is good for the throat, but I think lemon and other citrus fruits are too drying. If your throat feels gunky, try gargling with warm salt water instead.

If your AC or heater is running a lot, try running a humidifier as well to put some moisture back in the air, especially while you sleep. A steamy shower can moisten your vocal cords, too. Some singers use face or mouth steamers to inhale steam before a show.

Avoid smoke as much as possible. If you are a smoker, convince yourself to wait until after the show to indulge. Don't go to a smoky club the night before your show, but if that's unavoidable, run your humidifier afterwards while you sleep.

Exercise and stretching

The reason to exercise the day of the show is to get your breathing good and deep and to relieve any pre-show stress. You don't want to be tired for your show, so don't run a marathon that day. Instead, try a shorter run, swim, workout or yoga class to get yourself breathing deeply. If you run, walk, or swim, you can mentally rehearse your performance at the same time. Whatever you do, try not to grunt or otherwise tax your vocal cords while you exercise. A tennis game may feel great the day of a show, but try not to yell at your opponent as you play!
Stretching is also important. Any muscle that is tense should be loosened so that you can breathe easily and so that everything in your "vocal path," (throat, mouth, shoulders, and belly), feels relaxed. You

may be using your entire body during the performance, so full body stretches are in order. Take a beginning yoga class to learn some easy stretches, or just try neck rolls, shrugging your shoulders, lunges, and touching your toes.

Mental Preparation

This is when all the work you've done to build a positive attitude about yourself as a performer comes into play. Since nerves can arise as show time approaches, you may need more mental preparation than usual. You may want to meditate for a few minutes, repeating your performance mantra. You may want to mentally rehearse your show, anticipating what it will feel like when you're onstage, what you'll say, what the audience will look like, etc. If you've been able to research the venue in advance you can visualize the interior from the stage. You may want to do various methods you've found that quell any nerves that arise. I've found that the more I can anticipate the event and let any nervousness arise and dissipate in the hours *before* the show, the less nervous I am at the actual performance.

Vocal Warm Up

You may want to do a different vocal warm up on performance days and non-show days. On non-show days, you can build more vocal strength by singing more difficult exercises and songs. On performance days, just warm up your voice enough to get your range and tone in place, but save your voice for the show. How much to warm up and how much to rest your voice pre-show will vary greatly from singer to singer. Virtually all voices benefit from some warm up, unless you are sick and need to completely rest your voice. But some singers are good to go after ten minutes of warm up, and some need an hour. You'll need to experiment a lot with different exercises and warm up songs to find out what works best for you. If you warm up in the morning, your voice should stay warmed up for the rest of the day, unless you take a nap. My usual pattern is to warm up late morning or midday with exercises and songs, then only sing the easiest of sounds prior to the show. I've also found a few very easy warm up songs that I sing at a medium volume before heading out to the venue.

Some singers strain their voices more when they speak than when they sing. It's easier on your voice to speak at a soft volume and slightly higher pitched than normal— not as if you were Mickey Mouse, but as if you were talking to a baby. Whispering and yelling are both hard on the voice.

Actual Rehearsal

If you have the time and vocal strength, you can run some or all of your set. If you're short on time, you can just do the first couple of songs since that's when nerves are higher, and then the last couple of songs since they might be the most difficult. Or, just sing the beginnings and endings of each song, and what you'll say and do in-between. Those segues are often the least rehearsed part of the set.

If you feel that you should save your voice for the show, sing lightly or not at all as you run the set. Your brain will still remember what to do even if you don't audibly vocalize, and you'll reinforce your breathing, your memory of the lyric, your stage moves, your segues, and your lyric interpretation and sensory cues for each song. If at all possible, don't make last-minute changes to your song delivery. Late changes are the first thing to be forgotten when the adrenaline hits you, and you don't want to waste mental energy trying to remember something you haven't had a chance to fully rehearse.

Hair and clothing

Figure out in advance how much time you should allot to get dressed. This may be practically no time if you perform in jeans and a t-shirt, but it could be two hours if you have complicated hair, clothing and make-up needs. If you know it takes thirty minutes to get your hair just right, carve out the time. You'll feel more relaxed and confident. Many performers find that the act of putting on their performance clothes is how they transform into their stage persona. This may be a ritual that helps you to psychologically prepare for the show. To save time, have a bag already packed with a comb, lipstick, a bottle of water, and anything else you'll want to have with you at the venue.

What to take to the gig

If you aren't at the stage in your career where a manager, roadies or other assistants handle all extraneous details, make a checklist of everything you'll need at the show in advance. This might include your:

- Set list
- Business cards
- Mailing list sign-up sheet
- CDs to sell
- CD of backing tracks
- Clothing and makeup (if you're changing at the venue)
- Thermos of herbal tea
- Performance gear:
  Guitar or other instrument
  Extra strings
  Capo
  Mic
- Stage props you use in your set
- Breath mints

Use your checklist so you don't have to remember anything right before you leave for the venue. Pack as much as you can the night before. The breath mints are for after the show since singing can cause breath issues and you will be greeting fans. If you've never been to the venue, make sure to include a piece of paper with the address, clear directions for getting there, where to park, and the contact person's name.

15-30 minutes before the show

If you have a backstage in which to wait, you can do all the last-minute things that best help you prepare. Hopefully you will have had time for a full vocal warm up earlier in the day. Now, just make easy, relaxing sounds like humming or sighing as you focus on your breathing. Stretching will also relax you and get you breathing more deeply. You may want to close your eyes to focus on your breathing, repeat your positive attitude mantra, or simply gather your energy. If you're wound up with nerves, you can do all of the tension relieving methods detailed in the *Handling Stage Fright* chapter.

I'm the type of performer who has energy to spare just before a show, but some people are *too* relaxed before a performance. If that sounds like you, you'll want to rev up backstage by running in place, dancing, or singing or mouthing your most uptempo song.

Remember to keep your vocal cords hydrated with plenty of room temperature water.

Experiment with all of these elements on rehearsal and performance days to find out what works best for you. If you have a really great rehearsal or performance, take note of how much sleep you had, what your diet was that day, if you got any exercise and what kind, and anything else you think contributed to your success. Then repeat the pattern on another rehearsal or performance day to see if these things continue to make a difference. Be your own researcher as to exactly what helps you the most. Since everyone is different, don't take another singer's experience as gospel. Milk products are universally known as being bad for the singing voice, but I've found that I can have cereal with milk and then sing just fine. But if I drink coffee and sing I get hoarse in five minutes! Your job is to stay aware of anything that helps or hinders you as a singer and performer so you can set yourself up for success the day of a show. Knowing that you are taking care of yourself will boost your mood and confidence.

Also, take note of what seems to be absolutely essential for you to perform well. Some days you may go straight from your day job or tour bus to the show, so develop a short list of performance preparation essentials. That could mean a ten-minute nap or meditation, time for a run and shower, vocal warm up, or simply some time to think through your set.

When you learn which of these regimens works best for you, you might want to incorporate some or all them into the days preceding a show as well as the day of. Smart touring performers often go into training mode prior to a tour to get a head start on good pre-performance habits. They do the best they can to maintain these habits throughout the rigors of touring, and then relax their regimen when they are off the road.

Chapter 28:
After the Performance

Immediately after the performance

You might think that your work is done after each performance, and to a certain extent it is. Enjoy your performance high, feel satisfaction for a job well done, greet people backstage, and receive their compliments—these are the rewards for all of your hard work. There are just a couple of things to attend to along with your revelry.

Vocal warm-downs

You've just used your vocal cords in a very demanding way. Even singers with excellent technique may feel some tension in their jaws or throats after a performance. Those with less technical skill may feel considerable strain in the larynx or throat. Before you head out to celebrate with your friends, do some vocal warm-downs to get your voice and body back in the right place. If you don't, you might strain your voice further while talking after the show. Gently massage your jaw and the sides of your throat. Another way to relax your jaw muscles is to pretend you're chewing gum. If you also make some sloppy, relaxed noises as you do this, like saying "myum, myum, myum," you'll probably feel vibration, or resonance in your face. If not, repeat the sounds while mock chewing and shaking your head "No." Making sure you have good facial resonance is the other part of your warm-down, and most sloppy sounds with some M's in them will do that. You don't have to sing actual notes, just vocalize loosely on resonant sounds.

Mood maintenance

After coming down from the performance high, some artists find themselves plagued by the blues or dissatisfaction with their performance. Others find their mood sinking right after the performance if they feel that their performance or the audience response wasn't what they hoped for. Some artists feel their mood plunging or their self-doubt rising even if they gave a great performance! These feelings are very powerful, particularly after the adrenaline rush of performing. Many artists get into trouble with drinking or drugs as they try to numb these intense moods. There are several better ways to handle them.

If you often get a little down after a performance, try to schedule seeing friends or family right afterward so you have company. Being with loved ones can stave off the blues. Or, find an artist buddy to talk to after a performance and do the same for her.

Sometimes it's the lack of control in a performance that throws artists into a funk afterward, and the artist doesn't feel right until that's addressed. What can help is to sing by yourself to regain your connection with your artistic self. Singing in the car as you drive to meet friends might do the trick, but some artists feel better being by themselves after a show so they can sing and regain their feeling of control.

The important thing here is to notice if your mood often drops after a show, and to find out what brings you back to earth a bit more gently, whether that is spending time with others or alone. Also find out *how* you should spend time after the performance— whether doing something physical like dancing, singing a bit more, or vegging out feel best.

If your harsh inner critic is working overtime after a show, one way to quiet your mind is to tell yourself that you will evaluate your performance at a later time. Then actually do an evaluation the day after a show, when you can review your performance more clearly. This can work very well to silence your inner critic, but only if you follow through with an evaluation later on.

The next day evaluation

Just as you evaluated yourself during rehearsals, it's beneficial to evaluate your actual performances so that you stay aware of what is working and what could be improved. If it was a wonderful performance, you'll want to take note of everything that may have contributed to your success so that you can replicate it. If you've given a lackluster performance, try not to think "Oh, whatever," and put it out of your mind.

Congratulate yourself for giving the performance, and evaluate what went wrong. When you know exactly what the problems are you can address them. Knowing exactly what needs fixing can alleviate your thinking "I just sucked!"

At one point after playing a few less-than-perfect solo shows I realized that my guitar parts were too difficult for me to execute live. I played them fine during rehearsals, but during shows I made little mistakes that distracted me, probably because my focus was on singing. I stepped up my guitar practice, but it didn't help. Finally, I figured out slightly easier guitar parts. Bingo! My performances improved immensely.

Sometimes the problem has nothing to do with your talent or how much you rehearse. When I lived in the Bay Area my band had a couple of awful shows at clubs that had terrible sound systems. We were well rehearsed and in good form, but there was nothing we could do to improve the sound. Since these weren't premier showcase clubs, we stopped doing shows at them and found other venues. It simply wasn't worth it to torture ourselves and our fans with mediocre sound.

Get in the habit of doing these evaluations the day after a show, and if possible learn to do them quickly so you don't get bogged down and skip doing them. You'd then lose a valuable way to improve your future performances.

Post-Performance Evaluation, Part One

Rate these statements from 1 to 10. 1 is "I strongly disagree," and 10 is "I strongly agree."

I felt in control and able to focus, both vocally and physically. _____

Overall, I sang well. _____

My intonation was good. _____

My vocal tone was good and stayed consistent. _____

My accuracy and strength were good on both the highest and lowest notes. _____

I felt confident and not nervous. _____

My persona came across clearly and my performing intentions were clear. _____

My clothing looked good and was easy to move and breathe in. _____

I was happy with the sound in the monitor and main speakers. _____

My visual focus was good. _____

My mic technique was good. _____

My body movements were what I wanted them to be. _____

I stayed connected to the essence of each song. _____

I connected with the audience. _____

Post-Performance Evaluation, Part Two

1. If I was nervous:

a. How strong was it: mild, manageable, uncomfortable, paralyzing?

b. How long did the nervousness last?

c. Did anything ease the nervousness?

d. Did anything make it worse?

2. How was my overall mental attitude: positive or negative?

3. Did my attitude change during the course of the performance?
If yes:

a. What caused it to improve or worsen?

4. Was I able to focus or did I feel scattered and easily distracted?

5. Did my ability to focus change during the course of the performance?
If yes:

a. What caused it to improve or worsen?

6. Did I make any mistakes?   If yes:

a. Did I let the mistake disrupt the flow of my performance?

b. Was the mistake due to nervousness or not enough rehearsal?

7. Was I easily distracted?   If yes:

a. Were these distractions external (e.g. a noisy audience) or internal? (e.g. too many unwanted thoughts.)

8. Did anything else go wrong?

9. What songs went over the best?

10. Were there any songs that didn't work?

11. Were there any songs that were surprisingly difficult to sing?

12. Did the pacing of the show feel strong, or were there any "dead" spots?

13. Did anything I say go over really well?

14. Did anything I say *not* go over well?

15. Is there anything else that I could do to improve my next performance?

As you can see, Part Two of the evaluation digs a little more deeply into your performance. Your answers to both sections will help you find the areas that need some work, and also give you clues as to what helps you to give your strongest performance. It's also valuable to videotape and evaluate your live performances. For that you can use the evaluation checklist in the *Videotaping Yourself* chapter.

Don't beat yourself up about any areas of your performance that you think can be improved upon. Remember that there's a big difference between taking note of things you need to work on and telling yourself that you aren't good enough. The greatest performers are the ones who continually evaluate and improve every aspect of their performances.

As you progress as a performer you will undoubtedly become better at analyzing your shows and you may not need to do this extensive questionnaire each time you perform. Some kind of evaluation is still in order, though. It may be as simple as a quick mental check-in on how you felt, and what did and didn't work during the performance.

Chapter 29:
Tips from the Pros

I have a lot of very talented friends, so I gathered opinions from some of them about what helps them give a great performance. This group collectively has sung for thousands of people around the world, both solo and in bands. They've won awards, and performed on TV, radio, and in movies.

Our panel

Jon Rubin www.rubinoos.com: Jon's band the Rubinoos was one of the hottest power pop bands of the 70s (major label releases, top 40 airplay, tours galore, 16 Magazine teen idols), and are still going strong— they just got back from touring Japan.

Diana DeWitt www.phonorec.com: Diana is a top session singer in Nashville, last seen backing Neil Young on Saturday Night Live. She's sung everywhere, both singing her own songs and backing the likes of Amy Grant, Michael McDonald, and BB King.

Tom Kimmel www.tomkimmel.com: Tom is a renowned touring singer-songwriter with two major label and several indie releases to his credit. His songs have been covered by Linda Ronstadt, Johnny Cash, Joe Cocker, Shawn Colvin, Waylon Jennings, Randy Travis, the Spinners, and many more. A reformed rocker, these days he's usually on the road heading towards another solo acoustic show.

Cecily Gardner www.cecilygardner.com: Cecily has led numerous jazz, R&B and pop bands in California, touring as far as Europe and the Middle East. She has sung at weddings, festivals, conventions and clubs large and small, and recorded and appeared with everyone from Bobby McFerrin to Dianne Reeves. She's also a great voice coach if you're looking for one in Los Angeles.

Joyce Woodson www.joycewoodson.com: Joyce has toured the US, Wales and the UK, singing her original folk, swing and cowboy songs at festivals, bars, house concerts and everything in-between.

Kayre Morrison www.morasmodern.com/recordings-international.html: Kayre has sung the lead in regional and touring productions of Guys & Dolls, Singing in the Rain, Evita, and many other shows. She also sings with Mora's Modern Rhythmists Dance Orchestra.

Tim Buppert www.myspace.com/timbuppert: Tim is an A-list session and jingles singer in Nashville as well as a songwriter with cuts by Trisha Yearwood, among others. He's gigged throughout the South, and also is a rock-solid drummer.

Shelley Higgins www.clubboheme.com/shelleyhiggins.html: Shelley has sung in swing, a cappella, jazz, rock, and klezmer bands throughout California and North Carolina, and currently leads Club Boheme and the Magnolia Klezmer Band.

Kathy Hussey www.kathyhussey.com: A winner of the prestigious New Folk award at the Kerrville Folk Festival, Kathy has toured the US as a solo artist and is currently scoring her first movie.

Robert Sicular: Though not a performing singer, I wanted to include Robert because of his extensive experience as a stage actor. He has acted in major theater productions throughout the US for thirty years, playing the lead in Hamlet, Taming of the Shrew, and Richard II among numerous Shakespearean and modern plays.

Renee Hayes www.the-irrationals.com: Renee has sung in a cappella, Motown, R&B and gospel bands, has backed numerous singer-songwriters, has done loads of session work, and is a well-respected arts educator in the SF Bay Area.

Effective pre-performance regimens

Kayre Morrison:
I like a good, thorough warm up, vocal and physical. After doing some vocal exercises, I sing through at least part of the material I'll be doing in the performance. For me, it builds muscle memory of the song. If I get

distracted, I can usually depend on this to take me through the rest of the piece. I also try to find time to do a physical warm up, especially if I'm stressed about the show. I focus on stretching my back, neck, jaw, and upper extremities.

Kathy Hussey:
If I have the chance, I always try to do some yoga before a big performance. I also make a point of making sure I'm very well-hydrated and nourished— lots of water, good healthy food all day, and no dairy products for at least 24 hours.

Tom Kimmel:
I used to have a fairly elaborate pre-show ritual, but that's somehow simplified itself over the past several years. There are two things I need most (and build into my travel schedule as often as possible) on the afternoon of a show: a nap and a shower. I somehow seem to emerge a new man, and it's as if a new day has begun, a day in which my only real concern is doing a good performance. If time is really tight and a nap and/or shower isn't possible, then there are two activities that comprise my bottom line preparation: brushing my teeth and putting on a clean shirt!

Cecily Gardner:
I like to do yoga the day of a performance, an hour and a half practice if possible. It gets me centered and "into my body." Immediately before a show I often get into a flurry with set lists, band set-up, shuffling charts, etc, so I try to take a few minutes of quiet time to settle.

Renee Hayes:
What helps me before a show is warming my voice up with scales, breathing deeply, and singing a couple of songs— but not too many. I like to get to a venue early, before the audience comes in, so I can "claim" the space and make it feel as if the audience is walking into MY space. I also spend time right before the performance warming up, saying last minute words and doing a group hug with the other people in my performance ensemble— If I don't do this, I often don't feel as connected with them during the performance.

Tim Buppert:
I'm not the most disciplined of singers, so often I don't do anything, but if I can I do a couple of minutes of vocalizing: stretching the lower end of both the head and chest voice— it really helps. I also like to refrain from talking and make sure I get plenty of water.

Robert Sicular:
I would say getting by myself for at least a little while immediately prior to going on, to focus. I also, even after 100 performances of the same show, still go over most of my lines for accuracy and new discovery.

Jon Rubin:
I like preparation: rehearsal, scouting the venue, having confidence in my band and crew— it builds my confidence and makes me the most comfortable.

Joyce Woodson:
The day of the performance I try to steal a one-hour nap. If I'm following someone that evening I'll hum along with their last one or two songs on the sidelines. This warms up my voice and keeps the focus off of myself.

Diana DeWitt:
The better performances I have had come from warming up properly with my vocal exercise CD during the ride over for at least 20 minutes. I like arriving in plenty of time to catch a deep breath, settle in, and not be consumed with the anxiety of being late.

How to avoid phoning it in during a show

Jon Rubin:
Remember that you only live once and this ain't no dress rehearsal. If the gig is awful try to improve some aspect of the performance for yourself or your bandmates. If the gig is *really* awful and you don't care, have some fun. If all else fails, put yourself in the shoes of the audience and actually try to entertain them.

Shelley Higgins:
I let everything outside my body fade to black, listen only to my own breath, and connect with the message in the lyric.

Kayre Morrison:
There's really no time to think when you find yourself in this position: it isn't the time to examine WHY you're having trouble committing. You just have to trust your training and "fall" into the piece. With a song, you can usually do that easily by finding the meaning of the lyric. Once the show is over, you should spend some quiet time figuring out what went wrong and how to deal with it in future appearances.

Cecily Gardner:
It's easy to slip into auto-pilot, especially with songs I've sung many many times before. I remember that I picked (or wrote) that particular song for a reason— not just because I sound good singing it, but because the story resonated with me and moved me somehow. If I have to, I tap into an emotional place (a bit of "method acting" on the spot) to bring back the energy and emotion in the story.

Tom Kimmel:
Some nights are simply difficult for some reason. Perhaps there are distractions present— sound problems, for example, or distracting noises like traffic outside the venue— or maybe I'm fatigued and it shows up as forgetfulness— but everybody make mistakes, and some nights are "off nights." I actually talk to myself when I'm onstage. I'll say, "It's OK, Tom. It's just a mistake. You can shake it off. Just focus on what you're singing now.

Kathy Hussey:
I never lose my focus midway. For me, every show is a slow build-up to being focused and fully connected with the audience. It's a little like getting to know them. I like to try to communicate with an audience, and encourage them to communicate back, even in a big theater...I make a point to let them know that I am open to conversation and input and I'm not a character on a movie screen.

Robert Sicular:
If I do find myself wandering, I just make a quick mental reprimand: "You're a professional, dammit!" and focus back in.

Joyce Woodson:
If during a song I feel I'm just phoning in the performance, I'll check myself and be sure to re-create the story of the song in my mind line by line as I sing. I imagine the scenes as if in a full-color movie. This is where having songs in my set that I find interesting really helps!

Effective methods for easing stage fright

Kayre Morrison:
Well, this isn't too much of a problem for me in performance. By then, I've worked on the material and have a good concept of how it will be performed and received. That being said, I'm one of the most nervous auditioners ever! When I'm extremely nervous my voice quavers. Not so good for booking a job! I've found that NOT thinking about what I'm doing works best in that kind of high-pressure setting. At auditions, I do some deep breathing before entering the room, then STOP thinking about the "what ifs." I feel I audition best when I've prepared my song or piece well ahead of time.

Cecily Gardner:
Belly breathing!! When I am nervous, my breathing gets more into my chest (the fight-or-flight breath), it tightens my throat, raises my larynx and makes me even more nervous because then I can't sing easily the way I want to. When I return to a quiet belly breathing technique, not only do I have more breath to support my singing, but it calms the central nervous system, too.

Tom Kimmel:
I've done this enough that I understand that being nervous is part of the deal. If I'm asked (in an interview) if I still get nervous, I always respond, "If I weren't nervous, I'd really be nervous!"

There is of course a kind of nervousness that borders on panic. That doesn't occur for me often, but if I can sense it arising I can usually address it with a little quiet time for myself, a walk outdoors, and a pep talk with myself. "You're a pro," I might say. "You've done this a million times. It's going to be fine. Just focus on the songs— that' s the main thing."

But a little nervousness is, I think, a good thing. It lets me know that there's some spiritual energy.

Kathy Hussey:
 If you stress out about the feeling of being nervous, you just increase the physical reaction— if you simply allow yourself to feel nervous, accept it, and perform the best you can, it will just go away after a few songs.

Tim Buppert:
Jagermeister...well, honestly I don't get too nervous anymore. The more prepared you are the less nervous you get.

Shelley Higgins:
Before the show I do this: Deep breathing, then I imagine the moment after the show when my "real" life resumes. It will arrive when the last chord rings— how will that feel? When I am nervous, it feels like a great relief! Then I remember that I want to have gone somewhere else before that happens. I have access to a zone where the audience wants to go WITH me. We are on a little journey together that will end all too soon. Let's make the most of it!

Entering this little scenario helps me shake off my fears of judgment, failing to hit all notes and cues and making mistakes. That is what usually creates the nerves for me.

Another excellent performer friend of mine also added this:

What helps my nerves is a good ol' beta blocker. [See the *Handling Stage Fright* chapter for more on beta blockers.]

Additional tips

Cecily Gardner:
Pick your band to suit your music and your personality. Rehearsing isn't as important to me as having the right musicians to complement my style and "vibe" onstage. I have played with people who are reputed to be the

best of the best, but if they're arrogant to boot I don't enjoy the gig. They often don't make good team players, they'd rather show their skills than support the rest of the band and the singer. I'd rather have a humble and fun musician onstage who is perhaps slightly less skilled, but much more a part of the band.

Tom Kimmel:
Fourteen years ago I had an epiphany: the artist's role in community is one of service. Also, a certain amount of woodshedding is helpful— practice, planning, lessons, writing... the nuts and bolts of making music. I don't really like to practice, but I do care very much that I honor my gifts by doing a good job when I share.

Shelley Higgins:
I have gone to a gig thinking it was going to be a disaster because the day had been so stressful and I am late, and omigod, I think that mic cable has a short and I forgot to bring another one— then the gig is amazing. I have also been calm and collected and ready to give a great performance and had a mediocre evening.

Diana DeWitt:
It helps being almost *overly* rehearsed, but still leaving room for spontaneity and spirit so it feels like a second nature thing— and it's FUN! Also, I try to stay willing to open up and be vulnerable, so I can honor the song's story and whatever character I need to be in to draw the listener into the song.

Tim Buppert:
Make sure you're hearing well. Whether it's the headphone mix in the studio or the monitor mix onstage, you have to be able to hear well. Take the time you need to get it right and it'll save you time in the end. In the studio when I'm singing lead I tend to sing best with one side of the headphones off. If i have both sides on i tend to sing a little sharp. When singing harmony I usually have both sides on. I can't really explain the reason for this but I expect it has something to do with the doppler effect wherein the closer you are to a sound the higher its pitch.

Renee Hayes:
I think that it's impossible to be too prepared, but ultimately it's connecting with and conveying the love of your music and the message you want to impart that's the most important thing. I also think that it's crucial to have respect for the intelligence of your audience.

Robert Sicular:
Remember that it's FUN! Also, that the audience *wants* to like you. And never, never apologize for being onstage. And for me, it's about the collaborative effort: interaction, listening, playing together, truth, integrity. And FUN!

Kayre Morrison:
Again, be prepared. For me that might mean spending extra time dissecting the song/scene, working the piece in front of a mirror or on tape, prepping wardrobe, hair, makeup, and gear in advance. Anything that allows me to walk into the situation as confidently as possible is good. Also, get there early!

Kathy Hussey:
I once drove a long way to see one of my favorite performers who was doing a show on an outdoor stage in a theme park plaza. There wasn't any formal seating and people were just passing by and not really listening. I was, though, I was sitting on a little brick wall and looking forward to finally hearing her live. She was awful— she clearly didn't want to be there, and sang like she just wanted to get it over with. She lost a lot of respect from one huge fan who never bought another CD or sought out another live performance.

I have never forgotten that, and I ALWAYS perform as if there is at least one person in the audience who will be disappointed by anything but me giving it my ALL, because chances are very good that there is.

Jon Rubin:
Either have worked-up material for between songs, or, I think this is better, just be yourself and entertain people. I find that most of those things work out organically. There is nothing wrong with having worked-up bits. Knowing you have a backup plan if things go south may give one the confidence to try new things. I generally like to talk about current events and weird or mundane things that happened to me that week —

or I tell lies. Always be prepared to throw everything out the window and wing it.

Play live as much as possible. There is no substitute.

If you are not entertaining, at least to yourself and your immediate friends and family, maybe you're in the wrong business.

Did I mention preparation?

The more I love what I am doing the happier I am. The more I like the people I play with the happier I am. The happier I am, the better I am. Good advice: Try not to do gigs you hate.

Try to approach each gig as a new wonderful experience. Try to remember why you ever started doing this. Don't sweat the small stuff. It's all small stuff.

About the Author

Susan Anders has coached thousands of contemporary singers in the Bay Area, Los Angeles, and Nashville. Her vocal programs *The No Scales, Just Songs Vocal Workout*, *Harmony Singing By Ear*, and *Singing with Style* are being used by singers worldwide.

Susan has performed solo and in bands at huge festivals, tiny coffeehouses, on radio and TV, and everywhere in-between. Her former band Susan's Room released five albums, and she has also released two solo albums: *Release,* and *You Can Close Your Eyes*, a lullaby album. Susan was born and raised in Berkeley, California, and now lives with her husband Tom Manche in Nashville, Tennessee.